W9-CEE-643

What the experts say about *The Copyright Permission and Libel Handbook*

". . . a clear and accessible guide for publishing professionals."
—Robert Asahina, President and Publisher
Adult Publishing Group, Golden Books Family Entertainment

"An absolute must for every writer, author, and publishing bookshelf. In the complex and intimidating world of copyrights, Jassin and Schechter are able to make it readable and understandable."
—Jerrold R. Jenkins, Publisher
Independent Publisher and *Publisher Entrepreneur* magazines

"The lucid explanations of every aspect of a subject that confounds many make this book an indispensable tool for publishing professionals, writers, and students. Loaded with practical help and thoughtful commentary."
—Sandra Choron, literary agent, March Tenth, Inc.

"This book is an excellent guide to the complicated world of rights clearance. Clearly and concisely written, it should be required reading for anyone who wants to reproduce, or borrow from, an artist's or author's copyrighted work."
—Robert Panzer, Executive Director
Visual Artists and Galleries Association, Inc. (VAGA)

"This book takes the mystery out of the Byzantine world of copyright and libel. It could save readers a fortune in legal fees. Every author and publisher who is concerned about using other people's copyrighted material—or avoiding being sued for libel—should own a copy."
—Whitney North Seymour, Jr.
founder, The Small Press Center,
practicing lawyer (since 1950)

"Every book publisher needs a working knowledge of copyright infringement, defamation, and invasion of privacy. This ready reference contains the protection you need. Highly recommended."
—Dan Poynter, publishing consultant
and author of *The Self-Publishing Manual*

"Now there is a source that clearly explains, in understandable English, the very issues all authors and writers must address in today's legal climate. A savvy author avoids expensive trouble! Should be on the shelf of every writer and publisher."

—Dennis R. Reiff, President
D. R. Reiff Associates,
media perils insurance brokers

"An extremely valuable tool for publishing and multimedia professionals."

—Robert F. Abbanat, President
Engineered Multimedia, Inc.

"This handbook is comprehensive in scope and sorely needed in the ever-growing world of the Internet and the New Media in general. The insurance information in this book will be invaluable to readers."

—Ron Cohen, President
Near North Insurance Brokerage,
media perils insurance brokers

"A solid guide for everyone dealing in the writing/publishing industry. This book will be applauded not only as a fantastic reference, but also as a much-needed explanation of what copyright law is really intended for—the progress of art!"

—Bradley Kirkland, Chairman, CEO
AOL's *The Writer's Club*

The Copyright Permission and Libel Handbook

A Step-by-Step Guide for Writers, Editors, and Publishers

Lloyd J. Jassin

Steven C. Schechter

John Wiley & Sons, Inc.

New York • Chichester • Weinheim • Brisbane • Singapore • Toronto

This book is printed on acid-free paper. ∞

Copyright © 1998 by Lloyd J. Jassin and Steven C. Schechter. All rights reserved.
The authors claim no copyright in the Copyright Office materials reprinted in
Appendixes A and B.

Published by John Wiley & Sons, Inc.
Published simultaneously in Canada.

No part of this publication may be reproduced, stored in a retrieval system or
transmitted in any form or by any means, electronic, mechanical, photocopying,
recording, scanning or otherwise, except as permitted under Sections 107 or 108 of the
1976 United States Copyright Act, without either the prior written permission of the
Publisher, or authorization through payment of the appropriate per-copy fee to the
Copyright Clearance Center, 222 Rosewood Drive, Danvers, MA 01923, (508) 750-
8400, fax (508) 750-4744. Requests to the Publisher for permission should be addressed
to the Permissions Department, John Wiley & Sons, Inc., 605 Third Avenue, New
York, NY 10158-0012, (212) 850-6011, fax (212) 850-6008, e-mail:
PERMREQ@WILEY.COM.

Publisher's Note: This publication is designed to provide accurate and authoritative
information in regard to the subject matter covered. It is sold with the understanding
that the publisher is not engaged in rendering legal, accounting, or other professional
services. If legal advice or other expert assistance is required, the services of a competent
professional person should be sought.

Authors' Note: This book is not intended as legal advice. Because the law is not static,
and one situation may differ from the next, neither the authors nor the publisher can
assume responsibility for any actions taken based on information contained in this
book. Also be aware that the principles contained in this book are subject to exceptions
and qualifications, and may vary from state to state. Thus, when in doubt, seek legal
advice from an experienced publishing attorney, or err on the side of caution and
obtain permissions or an appropriate release.

Library of Congress Cataloging-in-Publication Data:

Jassin, Lloyd J.
    The copyright permission and libel handbook : a step-by-step
guide for writers, editors, and publishers / Lloyd J. Jassin, Steven
C. Schechter.
      p.   cm. — (Wiley books for writers series)
    Includes index.
    ISBN 0-471-14654-4 (paper : acid-free paper)
    1. Copyright—United States.   2. Libel and slander—United States.
I. Schechter, Steven C. II. Title. III. Series
KF2994.J37   1998
346.7304'82—dc21   97-25192

Printed in the United States of America

10 9 8 7 6 5 4 3 2 1

To my patient and loving wife, Beth, without whom this would not be possible

L.J.J.

To my friends and family for their support and their patience during the research and writing of this book

S.C.S.

Contents

5   What Copyright Doesn't Protect   54

6   Getting Permission   62

Part Two
The Libel Handbook

Acknowledgments

The authors wish to express their thanks and appreciation to the following individuals for their help and cooperation: Barbara Zimmerman (B/Z Permissions), Paul Basista (Graphics Artists Guild), Beth Jassin, Grace Miglio, Ronald Cohen (Near North Insurance Brokerage, Inc.), Jon Hutton and Ainslee Schreiber (summer associates), Jennifer Ross (legal assistant), Thomas J. McCormack, Maria Pallante (United States Copyright Office), Jamie Turton, and Robert Panzer (Visual Artists and Galleries Association). We would particularly like to thank our editors, PJ Dempsey and Chris Jackson (John Wiley & Sons), for their insight and encouragement.

How to Use This Book

This book is actually two books in one. Part One, "The Copyright Permission Handbook," provides step-by-step instructions on how to determine when permission is needed to use preexisting material in your work. It also discusses in depth how to locate the party who has the authority to grant you permission to use the work in question. Part Two, "The Libel Handbook," deals with liability for false information, or damaging facts, as well as invasions of privacy. It should be consulted after you have checked for copyright infringement issues and have obtained appropriate permissions.

We suggest you read the book cover to cover, keeping in mind that all of the principles contained in this book are subject to exceptions and qualifications. For quick-and-easy reference we've included convenient checklists, practical tips, real-life examples, model forms, and useful addresses and phone numbers that can save you countless hours. Following is a description of the content in each chapter.

Chapter 1, "Clearing Rights: An Overview," calls your attention to the many important and overlapping side issues involved in preparing a work for publication.

Chapter 2, "Copyright Basics," is a good starting point for understanding the permission process because without a copyright owner's permission, you cannot use the work. Because these principles (which are governed by federal copyright law) apply in virtually every situation, we recommend that you familiarize yourself with this material.

Like most rules, there are important exceptions to copyright law's basic tenets. For example, Chapter 3 introduces the *fair use* defense. While this is not technically an exception, if a use is a fair use, no permission is required. We'd be lying if we said there was a magic formula to help you distinguish a fair use from a foul use. However, by reading this chapter, you'll be in a much better position to make fair use judgments.

In Chapter 4, "What's in the Public Domain?" we explain why permission may still be needed to use certain types of public domain works. In addition, we explain how to tap the vast store of material available free (or for little money) in the public domain.

Chapter 5, "What Copyright Doesn't Protect," introduces other types of material, such as ideas, facts, theories, titles, and short phrases, which are not protected under copyright law.

In Chapter 6, "Getting Permission," we provide step-by-step instructions on how to secure permission, or *clear rights*, to use selected categories of works. This chapter, which is filled with convenient addresses and other useful information, provides practical advice on the whole permission process.

Chapter 7, "Dealing with Collaborators and Contributors," addresses important issues involving outside contributors, such as editors, graphic artists, photographers, and indexers. Whenever you pay someone to create something from scratch (as opposed to paying for a preexisting work), or you work with a collaborator, important issues relating to ownership, credit, and compensation arise. Avoid misunderstanding. Read this chapter first! If you don't, you may not get all that you've bargained for.

Chapter 8, "Multimedia Clearances," introduces the world of mixed-media clearances, providing an analysis of the complex ownership issues involved in licensing and content for new media.

Part Two, "The Libel Handbook," explains how you can minimize the risk of committing libel or invading someone's right of privacy by vetting (evaluating) your manuscript.

Chapter 9, "Basics of Libel Law," defines libel law and the basic elements of defamation. Bear in mind that libel law, which is constantly changing, is extremely complex.

Chapter 10, "How to Minimize Libel Claims," provides practical advice, procedures, and pointers on how to avoid libel claims. Because both fiction and nonfiction works can be libelous, fiction writers and their publishers should not skip over this chapter.

Chapter 11, "Basics of Publicity and Privacy," concerns two separate rights: (1) the right of publicity, and (2) the right of privacy. The right of publicity is the right of a person to control the commercial use of his or her identity. The right of privacy is a person's right to be left alone.

Chapter 12, "When and How to Obtain a Release," deals with the best (and cheapest) form of insurance against libel, invasion of privacy, and other publishing perils. While releases are not legally required, releases, or consent forms, are particularly useful if you intend to interview someone for a book or article.

Chapter 13, "Media Perils Insurance," talks about the defamation and intellectual property insurance policies that publishers (and authors) can obtain. Unfortunately, even a frivolous lawsuit costs money to defend. Fortunately, there are special policies that will pay the cost of defending your right to speak freely.

Bear in mind that the principles found in Part Two vary from state to state and are subject to rapid change. Thus, it is your responsibility to make certain that the principles contained in "The Libel Handbook" (and throughout this book) are current and apply to your situation.

Appendix A contains information on how to determine the copyright status of a work by investigating the Copyright Office catalogs and records. This is useful for determining whether a work is still in copyright, and for tracking down the party who has the authority to grant you permission to use a work or a portion of it.

Appendix B explains how to obtain frequently requested Copyright Office circulars and forms via a fax or over the Internet. It also provides instructions on how to access copyright registration and renewal certificates (helpful for finding out who owns the copyright to a work) on the World Wide Web.

Appendix C provides basic legal forms that you may adapt and reuse. Before using, or altering, the forms (or any standard form), we advise that you consider having them reviewed by a qualified attorney to make sure they comply with local state law and the facts of your particular situation.

Appendix D contains sample disclaimers for both fiction and nonfiction works. With a work of fiction, perhaps the best disclaimer is the prominent use of the word "novel" on the cover of a book.

Appendix E contains a list of trade and industry groups. If you cannot determine who owns a particular work, you might want to check with the relevant group.

CAUTION Due to the rapid pace with which the law changes, this book cannot replace the advice of an experienced attorney. However, it is our hope that by understanding the fundamental legal issues we've raised, you can anticipate, and therefore avoid, many potential legal problems. If any red flags pop up, it is our hope that you will seek the advice of a competent professional, or that you will err on the side of caution and seek appropriate permissions and releases.

Introduction

When do I need permission to use someone else's copyrighted work? What are the consequences of not getting permissions? What is a personal or property release? What do I do if I can't find the owner of copyrighted material? Are public domain works free for the taking? Are titles copyrightable? Do I need permission to publish interviews? Who owns the copyright to work I've commissioned? Do dead celebrities have rights? What is fair use?

This book is for you if you ever wish to draw on the writings of other people, or if you intend to use someone else's artwork, photographs, or protected images, in your own written (or multimedia) work. It is also for you if you are an author or publisher concerned about libel and other claims that can be made against you for things you publish.

Our goal is to help you to think strategically about the permission process and to minimize the risks associated with the creative process. To do so, you must keep in mind that intellectual property rights run like invisible threads through all literary and artistic works. As an author (or publisher), you have a duty to see all of these individual strands as well as the fabric as a whole. If you do not, you run the risk of infringing on someone else's property rights.

For this reason, it is important to be aware of the laws that affect creators. Copyrights guarantee that creators receive payment for new ways of expressing fundamental ideas and theories. Trademarks permit people to distinguish between goods (and services) that might otherwise be indistinguishable. The right of publicity gives well-known individuals the right to exploit the value of their celebrity. Libel laws protect people's reputations. Scratch the surface of any creative work, and any one—or all—of these rights, or risks, may be present.

While the First Amendment may appear unconditional on its face, the right to speak and write freely has never been absolute. Unfortunately, too many projects are stillborn or abandoned because not enough thought was given to the legal issues that affect authors, artists, and other creative people. Often, writers reveal their confusion about the permission process by either

1

seeking permission when none is required or borrowing what is not theirs to take.

While it is best to have an experienced attorney review your work for potential legal problems, this book will help to alert you when you need a permission (or release) and will show you how to go about getting one. As an author, editor, or publisher, you will find this book an enormous help. You should consult it every time you either borrow someone's creative expression or quote or depict a real-life person in your literary work. If you identify a potential problem, obtain permission (or release), or seek the advice of an experienced publishing attorney.

If you'd like to be kept up-to-date on the issues discussed in this book, you can link directly to the following website: www.copylaw.com. We welcome your insights and suggestions for future editions. Please feel free to write us at the following addresses:

Lloyd J. Jassin
Law Offices of Lloyd J. Jassin
P.O. Box 3444
Grand Central Station
New York, NY 10163

Steven C. Schechter
39-26 Broadway
Fair Lawn, NJ 07410

Part One

The Copyright
Permission Handbook

1

Clearing Rights: An Overview

If you intend to use someone's copyrighted work, unless the use is considered a fair use, you must obtain that person's written permission. Under federal law, only the copyright owner or someone acting with the owner's authority, such as a publisher, can grant you that permission. Without written permission, you expose yourself to legal risks. While not every unauthorized use of a copyrighted work is an infringement, whenever you include another person's words, illustrations, photographs, charts, or graphs in your own work, you must be sensitive to the risk of infringing on someone's copyright.

In certain instances, no permission is needed to quote or to reproduce another person's work. For example, copyright does not apply to works in the public domain, which includes both works for which the copyright has expired and many U.S. government works (see Chapter 4, "What's in the Public Domain?"). Copyright also recognizes limitations for fair uses of copyrighted works, although the exact limits of fair use cannot be quantified (see Chapter 3, "Fair Use").

Bear in mind that most publishers will insist on receiving copies of the written permissions you obtained before they publish your work. While not all material will require written permission, without appropriate permissions, your manuscript is technically unpublishable.

1.1   Types of Clearances

There are two types of clearances—copyright permissions (or licenses) and releases. *Copyright permissions* give you the right to use a copyrighted work owned by someone else for a specified purpose. *Releases* are clearances from living people, allowing you to use their name, likeness, or identifying characteristics in a work. Unlike copyright permissions, releases are not usually required by publishers. However, they immunize you from potential liability.

1.1.1 Copyright Permissions

When you obtain permission to use a literary (or other creative) work, you are obtaining permission from the person who owns the copyright to use the work for a specified use, defined by contract. In plain English, a *permission* is a license to do something that you couldn't do without such a license.

A permission license can cover the entire scope of copyright, or it can be limited to a particular medium, market, language, territory, or period. While you can't always get what you want (e.g., world rights, in all languages, in all media, whether now known or hereinafter invented, in perpetuity) for the price you are willing to pay, you must obtain sufficient rights to market your work in its primary market and medium. Importantly, you must obtain all rights you've promised to deliver to your publisher.

The license or permission grant that you receive should also define how much (amount or portion) of the work can be used, and whether the grant extends to reprintings, revisions, or other versions. To avoid misunderstanding, the grant of rights should be drafted clearly so there is no ambiguity, and signed by the person granting you permission.

Licenses can be given on either an exclusive or nonexclusive basis. If the license is *exclusive*, the owner cannot give anyone else what he or she gave to you. Exclusive licenses, therefore, are much more valuable and costly than nonexclusive licenses. Permissions are generally *nonexclusive* licenses, which means that one or more individuals can exercise the same privilege at the same time. Therefore, if an owner of a photograph licenses you the nonexclusive right to reprint a photograph, the owner remains free both to publish the photograph elsewhere and to permit others to do so.

1.1.2 Releases

Releases (or consent forms) are agreements not to bring any claims against the person requesting the release. Unlike copyright permissions, which are affirmative grants of rights, a release is a promise *not* to sue or *not* to exercise certain rights. For example, the subjects of interviews can sign releases agreeing not to sue for invasion of their rights of privacy or publicity or for libel. Simply stated, the *right of privacy* is the right to be left alone. The *right of publicity*, a related concept, is a person's right to benefit from her or his own celebrity. A *libelous statement*, on the other hand, is any false statement, including a misquote (innocent or not), that injures a living person's reputation. While not always required by publishers, releases are your best (and cheapest) form of insurance.

Releases reduce risk. For example, if you use another person's name, photograph, likeness, or even voice, for commercial purposes, without that person's prior consent (or in the case of a minor, the consent of a parent or legal guardian), you may be liable for damages for invasion of privacy or publicity. Similarly, whenever you publish or republish a work that contains a false statement of fact about someone, you place yourself at risk of being sued for libel.

A well-drafted release will protect you against claims for copyright infringement, libel, invasion of privacy, and other legal perils. Such a release will also allow you to alter or reuse the original material, whether a quote or a photograph, without having to go back to the original subject for permission.

1.2   When Must You Request Permission?

Generally, you must obtain a copyright permission whenever (1) you use a substantial or material portion of a copyrighted work, or (2) you use any portion of it that might harm the market for the original. Under the law of fair use, an author may—without permission—use short direct quotations from a work, *provided* it is for purposes of criticism, comment, news reporting, scholarship, or research. Unfortunately, there are no mechanical rules to define what is a fair use and what is a foul use. Using even a very short but important passage from a larger work may constitute infringement. Moreover, highly creative works—such as fiction, fanciful prose, poems, song lyrics, and photographs and other visual works—are not, as a rule, friendly to fair use interpretations (see Chapter 3, "Fair Use").

TIP	Secure permission *before*, not after you use someone's copyrighted material. Last-minute negotiations are always more costly. Moreover, copyright owners are under no obligation to grant you permission. If you are denied permission, you must revise your work accordingly.

1.3   When Must You Obtain a Release?

Releases fall into two categories: right of publicity, or "model" releases, and interview releases.

1.3.1   Right of Publicity Releases

You *must* obtain a release whenever you use a person's name, picture, likeness, or other identifying characteristic (including voice) in a commercial setting. These releases are sometimes called "model releases." In this instance, the purpose of the release is to protect against both a lawsuit based on invasion of privacy or publicity and, to a lesser extent, a libel suit (see Chapter 9, "Basics of Libel Law," and Chapter 11, "Basics of Publicity and Privacy").

The use of the image of a public figure or celebrity on the cover of an unauthorized biography is generally considered an editorial use. You do not need a release if an image is being used for news or editorial purposes. However, the further you move away from legitimate social or political commentary, or the rendition of historical facts, the greater the need for a release. Even if you do not need a release from the person depicted in a photo, you will need permission from the photographer who took the picture. That is because copyright law, not the laws of privacy and publicity, governs the use of artwork and photography. Properly worded, a release may also protect you from becoming embroiled in a libel suit.

TIP While most books—and publishing companies—are commercial enterprises, courts usually treat books about newsworthy subjects, and subjects of general public interest, as noncommercial editorial uses protected by the First Amendment. If, however, the primary message of a book is to "buy" something, regardless of any incidental social message, the book will be treated as a commercial advertisement. Thus, the use of photos of celebrities in a "personality" calendar to promote commercial products or services (e.g., a bank calendar), for example, would *not* be an editorial use.

Also, most stock picture agencies, or picture archives, license editorial rights only. If an image contains a VIP or other celebrity, and a commercial use is planned, you must obtain a right of publicity release from the celebrity or from the celebrity's estate—yes, dead celebrities *do* have rights.

Obtaining a license to use a celebrity's name or likeness to promote a product or service is generally a matter of intense negotiation, involving agents and attorneys. Due to their complexity, the legal and business issues involved in securing a celebrity's right of publicity or endorsement are beyond the scope of this book.

Although private property (e.g., pets, cars, and buildings) does not enjoy a right of privacy, if you intend to use an image that contains recognizable subject matter for trade or advertising purposes, it is prudent to obtain a property release from the property owner, or the owner's agent. Like a model release, a signed property release will protect you against accusations that you have used the object for purposes of trade or advertising without the owner's permission.

TIP   Even if you've secured consent from the subject of a photograph to use her or his likeness, you still need permission from the copyright owner of the photograph to reprint the actual photograph. While the subject of the photograph can license you the right to exploit his or her likeness, only the photographer can license the use of the particular photograph.

1.3.2   Interview Releases

While the words "you can quote me on that" might sound reassuring, some state laws require a written consent for such a waiver to be valid. When you interview a person for an article or a book, and you want to quote from that interview, several possible legal issues are raised, including (1) copyright infringement, (2) right of privacy, (3) libel, and, in certain circumstances, (4) breach of contract, either for publication of statements made off the record or for use of quotes beyond the interviewee's consent.

One way to deal with these potential media perils is to obtain written consent before publication (see Appendix C, Form B, "Release Form for Interview"). Of course, getting a written consent is not always feasible, but you can probably get the subject of your interview to consent either on tape or in front of witnesses. Nonetheless, while written consent is not mandatory, written permissions and releases are important. Without written permission, if there's ever a dispute, the courts—not the parties—may have to decide the scope of the rights granted. Also, most publishers require written copies of permissions with delivery of your final work or manuscript. As a general rule, publishers look at releases as optional.

2

Copyright Basics

Copyright is a property right. It gives authors the sole right to control the reproduction of their creative works. The basic principle of copyright law is that the author (or authors) of a work owns the copyright to that work. If you want to use a song lyric or some inspired prose from another author in your own work, you need a complete understanding of copyright law. Lacking such understanding is the surest way to turn the creative process into a costly and embarrassing copyright mess.

For one thing, having a basic understanding of copyright law is fundamental to the permission process. Such an understanding will allow you to trace copyright ownership and to determine the copyright status of a work, including whether it is in the public domain or otherwise exempt from copyright protection. In this way, you can accurately address your permission requests to the copyright owner.

The law of copyright was enacted by the U.S. Congress and, unlike libel law, applies in all fifty states. The Copyright Act, which has been revised twice in the past 100 years, is the key to understanding the legal protection given to creative works. Current copyright law in the United States is based on the 1976 Copyright Act, which took effect on January 1, 1978.

2.1   What Is Copyright?

Copyright is a bundle of exclusive rights that provides authors of original literary, musical, dramatic, and artistic works with the sole right to authorize (or prohibit) the following uses of their copyrighted works:

- To reproduce all or part of the work
- To make new (derivative) versions
- To distribute copies by selling, renting, leasing, or lending them

- To perform (e.g., recite, dance, or act) the work publicly
- To display the work publicly, directly or by means of film, TV, slides, or other device or process

The first three rights are violated when anyone copies, excerpts, adapts, or publishes a copyrighted work without permission. In rare cases, an author may dedicate a work to the public domain, but unless the facts prove otherwise, you should assume that all original works published less than 75 years ago in the United States are protected by copyright.

2.2   What Does Copyright Protect?

Copyright protects only the original expression found in an author's work. *Expression* refers to the way in which an author describes, expresses, or illustrates something. Copyright does not protect ideas, concepts, procedures, principles, or discoveries revealed in an author's work. However, under certain circumstances, the way in which those noncopyrightable elements are selected and arranged may be entitled to protection as a collective work, which is explained in Section 2.8.

2.3   What Does the Term Author Mean?

Unless a work is considered a work for hire (explained in Section 2.14), the term *author* refers to writers, artists, photographers, composers, software programmers, and other creators of expressive materials. For copyright purposes, an author does not have to be a living person. For example, under appropriate conditions a corporation or partnership can be an author. In the case of a work for hire, the hiring party, not the actual creator, is considered the author of the work (see Chapter 7, "Dealing with Collaborators and Contributors").

2.4   What Entitles a Work to Copyright Protection?

Three conditions must exist before a work will be protected by copyright:

1. It must be "original."
2. It must be "fixed" in some tangible form, with the authority of the author.
3. It must fall within a special category of "eligible" works.

For copyright purposes, "original" simply means that the author did not directly copy from another source. A work does not have to be novel or aesthetically pleasing to be protected. Provided there is a modicum of creativity, and a work isn't copied, just about everything is copyrightable in this sense.

"Fixed" means that you can read or view the work either directly or by using some kind of device. For these reasons, copyright does not protect (1) extemporaneous speeches or improvisational performances that have not been recorded, or (2) works recorded without the authority of the author. For example, if a member of an audience audiotapes an extemporaneous speech without the speaker's permission, the speech most likely will not be protected under federal copyright law, although it might be protected under state law.

"Eligible" works must contain at least some minimal amount of creativity. Certain categories of material—including ideas, procedures, systems, methods of operation, concepts, principles, and discoveries—are not protected by copyright (see Chapter 5, "What Copyright Doesn't Protect").

2.5   Is Registration a Prerequisite to Copyright Protection?

A common misconception is that you must register a work with the U.S. Copyright Office for it to be protected by copyright. Under present law, copyright exists *automatically* from the moment a work is fixed in a tangible medium of expression. Therefore, registration with the Copyright Office is not necessary, although there are advantages to prompt registration.

2.6   What Types of Works Are Protected by Copyright?

Both published and unpublished works are entitled to copyright protection. Because creators are constantly finding new ways to express themselves, copyright easily adapts to new technologies and media. Therefore, the fact that something has been distributed anonymously over the Internet does not deny it copyright protection.

Among the categories of copyrightable works are:

- Literary works, including books, newspapers, well-developed literary characters, diaries, manuscripts, poetry, catalogs, brochures, ads,

directories, encyclopedias, electronic databases, and computer programs
- Musical works, including accompanying words (e.g., songs, advertising jingles)
- Dramatic works, including any accompanying music (e.g., plays, operas, monologues)
- Pantomime and choreographic works (e.g., mime, ballet, jazz and modern dance)
- Pictorial, graphic, and sculptural works (e.g., photographs, prints, art reproductions, maps, charts, cartoon characters, diagrams, drawings, statues, dolls)
- Motion pictures and other audiovisual works (e.g., movies, TV programs, interactive multimedia works)
- Sound recordings (e.g., recordings of music, words, or other sounds)
- Architectural works (e.g., actual building structures, plans, drawings)

Two additional categories of copyrightable works fall within one or more of the preceding categories: derivative works (based on other works) and compilations, which are discussed more fully in Sections 2.7 and 2.8, respectively. The key point to remember when dealing with derivative works and compilations is that you are dealing with multiple layers or elements of copyrightable material. Care must be taken to consider rights in each layer or component part of a derivative work or compilation.

2.7   What Is a Derivative Work?

A *derivative work* is a new work based on one or more existing works. Derivative works are sometimes referred to as "new versions" or "adaptations." Common examples of derivative works include: a revised edition of a book, a sequel, an English-language translation of a Greek classic, a motion picture based on a novel, or, conversely, a novelization of an original motion picture.

You can make a derivative work only with the permission of the underlying work's copyright owner. Similarly, to obtain permission to use a portion of a derivative work, you must identify all of the holders of the rights connected with that work. To do so, you must analyze the source of the original material, as well as the source of any new material added later or appearing for the first time.

2.7.1   What Does a Derivative Work Copyright Protect?

A derivative work is entitled to its own separate copyright. However, the author of a derivative work can claim copyright ownership only in the fresh layer of new material he or she has contributed, provided it is different enough from the original to be considered a new work. Minor changes such as copyediting changes, or helpful suggestions, are not generally copyrightable and do *not* give rise to a derivative work. The copyrights for that new material are independent of—and do not enlarge the scope, duration, or ownership of—any copyright in the preexisting material. As a result, the author of a new work based on a public domain source can protect his or her work, even though the underlying work is out of copyright. For practical information (and illustrations) on working with derivative works based on public domain materials, see Chapter 4, "What's in the Public Domain?"

TIP	If you want to use an entire derivative work, you will need permission from both the owner of the underlying work (provided it is in copyright) and the owner of the derivative work.

2.8   *What Is a Compilation?*

A *compilation* is a copyrightable work that is the result of bringing together or arranging preexisting material (regardless of whether that material is protected by copyright) in an original—or nonobvious—way. Copyright protection is based on the original selection, coordination, or arrangement of the material, not the copyright status of the preexisting material itself.

There are two types of compilations: (1) fact compilations, and (2) collective works. A *fact compilation* is created by arranging public domain information, such as names and addresses or other data, in some minimally creative way. Common examples of fact compilations are electronic databases, directories, almanacs, price lists, and catalogs. The point at which you infringe a compilation will depend on the nature of the compilation, and how much you've appropriated. However, taking discrete bits of pure data, or information, from a fact compilation does not, under current U.S. law, infringe the copyright in that work. It is important, however, to distinguish pure facts from estimates or guesses, the latter of which may be protected by copyright (see Chapter 5, "What Copyright Doesn't Protect").

A *collective work* is a special type of compilation created by arranging copyrightable elements in a single work. Common examples are poetry anthologies, encyclopedias, newspapers, and magazines. The copyright in each separate contribution to a collective work is distinct from the copyright in the larger collective work and, as a rule, belongs to the author of that separate contribution. If you want to use more than one contribution to a collective work, you will need permission from each separate contributor. However, as a general rule, you will not need permission from the owner of the collective work.

2.9 What's the Difference between Ownership of a Copy and Copyright Ownership?

Copyright law makes an important distinction between ownership of a particular copy of a work and ownership of the copyright interest embodied in that work. By purchasing a painting or photograph, or any other copyrighted work (including this book), you do not obtain any rights in that work's copyright.

Without a formal transfer of copyright ownership, the purchaser of a painting or photograph cannot reproduce or adapt that work without the copyright owner's permission. Under copyright law, artists and other copyright owners have continuing rights to their works, even after they sell, or give away, their only copy.

2.10 What Are Split Copyrights?

Any of the exclusive rights that make up a copyright can be subdivided, or split, into smaller and smaller pieces and then transferred to one or more parties. Just think about the way books are marketed. In addition to book rights, there are audio rights, foreign translation rights, performance rights, film adaptation rights, and even future technology rights. Each exclusive right is jealously guarded and, as a rule, sold piecemeal to one or more persons to maximize the author's return. The ways in which the copyright pie can be sliced is almost endless.

A copyright owner may limit any (or all) of the rights granted to another by (1) time, (2) geography, (3) language, or (4) type of use. Rights can even be split by market segment or channels of distribution (e.g., hardcover vs. paperback rights). Copyrights are infinitely divisible. Bear in mind that rights are seldom sold, licensed, or transferred in their totality or nonspecifically. As a rule, the person granting the rights retains any right not expressly sold or otherwise transferred. When requesting copyright permissions, remember that there is no such thing as one-stop shopping. If rights are split among two or more parties, you may need to go to more than one source to obtain clear permission.

2.11 How Do You Determine Who Owns a Copyright?

Determining who owns the copyright to a particular work is crucial to the permission process because only the author, or someone claiming rights through the author (e.g., a publisher), can grant you permission to use that work. With two exceptions (works made for hire and U.S. government works), the presumption is that the creator (or creators) of a work owns the copyright in that work. Of course, the original author is always free to sell or transfer his or her rights to another.

2.12 How Are Copyrights Sold or Transferred?

Because copyright is a property right, the owners of a copyright may sell, transfer, lease, license, or bequeath (by will) their copyright interest in whole or in part to one or more different individuals or groups. According to the Copyright Act, if a copyright owner wants to sell or transfer an exclusive right, that transaction must be *in writing* and must be *signed* by the owner of the rights being sold or transferred. Therefore, an oral grant of exclusive rights is not valid. However, once an exclusive right is sold or transferred, the new owner steps into the shoes of the previous owner and enjoys all the benefits of copyright ownership—including the right to grant permission requests and sue for infringement.

Permission to quote from a copyrighted work is almost always given on a *nonexclusive basis*, which means that more than one party can exercise that right at any given time. A nonexclusive license, however, is not a transfer of copyright ownership. Therefore, the recipient does not have the right to sue for infringement. Unlike an exclusive license, a nonexclusive license can be granted orally (or implied by the owner's conduct).

If a copyright has been sold or transferred, you must obtain permission from the most recent copyright owner. However, if you obtain permission from a copyright owner, and the owner later assigns the copyright to someone else, the new owner cannot revoke your permission, if the permission is both nonexclusive and in writing.

2.13   Where Can I Find a Written Record of the Current Copyright Holder?

While locating the rights holder may be as easy as examining the work you want to use, the name of the copyright owner at the time the work was published is not necessarily the name of the current copyright owner. Since copyrights can be sold, or transferred, locating a current rights holder may involve some detective work. If a work has been registered with the Copyright Office, you can probably locate the copyright owner, or the party with the authority to grant you permission, by obtaining a copyright registration or assignment search. Unfortunately, recordation of copyright assignments is voluntary, so there may not be a record of the current transferee on file with the Copyright Office. See Section 6.5, "What Do I Do If I Still Can't Locate the Rights Holder?" for more information.

2.14   Who Owns the Copyright to a Work Made for Hire?

A work made for hire (or "work for hire") is the most important exception to the basic rule that the creator of a work owns the copyright in his or her work. If a work is a work for hire, the hiring party, *not* the original creator of the work, is considered the author. As a result, the hiring party enjoys all of the benefits of copyright ownership—including the right to grant permissions and to sue for infringement.

Works for hire arise in two limited situations:

1. Works created by employees within the scope of their employment
2. Specially commissioned works done by invitation, such as through freelance contracts, *provided* certain conditions, discussed below, are satisfied.

It bears emphasizing that before a specially commissioned work will be considered a work for hire, the creator and the hiring party must sign a special work for hire agreement, *and* the work must fall within one of nine specific categories of works listed in the Copyright Act. As we discuss more fully in Chapter 7, "Dealing with Collaborators and Contributors," if you pay an independent contractor (e.g., ghostwriter, illustrator, or designer) to create a copyrightable work on your behalf, unless there is a *prior* written agreement, your rights to use that material may be extremely limited. If you work or engage in contracts with other creative people, we urge you to read Chapter 7.

2.15   What Is a Joint Work?

A *joint work* is a work prepared by two or more individuals, with the intention that their separate contributions be merged into a single work. Absent an agreement to the contrary, both authors own the work jointly and equally. Sometimes, when a work fails to qualify as a work for hire, the courts may infer a joint work from the parties' behavior.

Because coauthors are equal owners, either author can grant you permission to use the work. Joint works are discussed more fully in Chapter 7, "Dealing with Collaborators and Contributors."

2.16   How Long Are Copyrights Protected?

When copyright protection expires, a work is said to be in the *public domain*. If a work is in the public domain, anyone can use it without infringing the copyright, as the copyright no longer exists. Unfortunately, it is not always easy to tell whether an older work is still protected by copyright. To determine whether a work is protected by copyright, you must know both when the work was copyrighted and the identity of the author. Different rules apply to works created before January 1, 1978, and those created after that date. Pre-1978 works are governed by the 1909 Copyright Act (the "old" Copyright Act). Works created after 1978 are governed by the 1976 Copyright Act (the "new" Copyright Act). Unless you know otherwise, you should assume that any work created within the past 75 years is protected by copyright.

2.16.1   Old U.S. Copyright Law (works created before January 1, 1978)

The old U.S. Copyright Act (enacted in 1909) covers anything created before January 1, 1978. The maximum term of copyright protection for works *published* or *registered* before January 1, 1978, is 75 years. Under the old (1909) Copyright Act, which still governs pre-1978 works, copyright lasted for a first term of 28 years. During the last (28th) year of the first term, the copyright was renewable for an additional period of 28 years (later extended to 47 years). So a work originally copyrighted in 1924, and properly renewed, would remain protected through the end of 1999. After 1999, that work would fall into the public domain.

When the copyright laws changed in 1976, the law kept the renewal system for works still in their first term of copyright on January 1, 1978. In 1992, however, Congress amended the Copyright Act to provide for automatic renewal of works copyrighted between January 1, 1964, and December 31, 1977. Before enactment of the automatic renewal law, if an author (or assignee of the author) failed to renew within certain strict time limits, the work fell into the public domain, and all copyright protection was lost. At present, works already in the public domain for failure to renew still remain in the public domain, despite the 1992 amendment.

2.16.2   New U.S. Copyright Law (works created after December 31, 1977)

The new U.S. Copyright Act (enacted in 1976) covers anything created on or after January 1, 1978. As of this writing, the term of copyright protection in the United States is the life of the individual author plus 50 years for works created after January 1, 1978. With joint works, copyright protection lasts for the life of the longest surviving joint author plus 50 years. Works for hire, anonymous works, and pseudonymous works are protected for 75 years from the date of publication or 100 years from creation, whichever is shorter. If the author's name is revealed after publication, the normal life-plus-50-years rule or the work-for-hire rule then applies. So a novel written by Alex Author, written in 1997, would be protected for 50 years after Alex Author's death. For a more detailed explanation of copyright duration, see Chapter 4, "What's in the Public Domain?"

2.17   What Is Copyright Infringement?

Copyright infringement is not the failure to give someone proper credit (that's plagiarism). You can plagiarize a work in the public domain by passing it off as your own work. Copyright infringement is an unlawful appropriation—or unauthorized reproduction—of material protected by copyright. A *copyright infringer* is anyone who, without permission, exercises any of the exclusive rights granted to authors under the Copyright Act.

To show copyright infringement, two things must be proven:

1.   Ownership of a valid copyright
2.   Actual copying (as opposed to independent creation)

Copyright infringement occurs when there is unlawful copying of protected elements of a work protected by copyright. In addition, the amount borrowed must be more than trifling.

Because there is usually no smoking gun, or direct evidence of copying, indirect evidence is usually used to prove that copying occurred. Copying can be inferred if the defendant had an opportunity to view the copyright owner's work, and if there is *substantial similarity* between the two works that cannot be explained by mere coincidence.

2.17.1   Is It Copyright Infringement to Use Someone's Ideas?

Because copyright does not protect ideas and facts, copying alone is not enough to prove copyright infringement. To prove copyright infringement, a copyright owner must show that the infringer has copied *protected* material. When courts are asked to determine whether infringement has occurred, they disregard noncopyrightable elements (such as ideas and facts) and compare the copyrightable elements of the works.

Unfortunately, there is no simple test that can clearly distinguish unprotected ideas from protected expression. Each case must be decided on its own particular facts. However, where there are only limited ways of expressing a particular idea, courts will sometimes find the expression uncopyrightable. For example, one court denied copyright protection to a pamphlet explaining how to reorganize insurance companies, holding that to "prohibit similarity of language would have the effect of giving the copyright owner a monopoly over his idea." Similarly, a one-paragraph factual account in a reportorial style of the causes of the Industrial Revolution is unlikely to be copyright protected, because of the minimal amount of creativity involved. Where fact and expression merge, such as in the portrayal of factual truths, copyright protection is said to be extremely "thin." Nonetheless, a second author cannot copy or closely paraphrase the words that the first author used to describe or embellish his or her theories or ideas.

2.17.2   What Does It Take to Prove Copyright Infringement?

The two keys to an infringement suit are (1) proof of substantial similarity between the two works, and (2) evidence that the infringer took the plaintiff's protected expression.

At the risk of oversimplification, the following is an overview of the standards used to determine copyright infringement for different categories of works. Be aware, however, that every case is decided on its particular facts, so there are no hard-and-fast rules.

2.17.2.1   Ideas

As discussed, an author's copyright monopoly does not extend to the ideas contained in his or her work. Ideas are part of the public domain, and we can all build on them. Because the objective of copyright law is to further the progress of art and science, ideas are not protected by copyright law. That is, the protection of ideas would stifle, not encourage, creativity.

As stated in Section 102 of the 1976 Copyright Act, "In no case does copyright protection for an original work of authorship extend to any idea, procedure, process, system, method of operation, concept, principle, method of operation or discovery, regardless of the form in which it is described, explained, illustrated, or embodied in such work." However, the form of expression of ideas and their arrangement and selection are copyrightable. *Always bear in mind that copyright protection extends only to an author's expression of facts, not the facts themselves* (see Chapter 5, "What Copyright Doesn't Protect").

2.17.2.2   Factual Works

Because facts, like ideas, are not protected by copyright, authors of factual works are afforded a narrow range of protection. Facts and theories unearthed during research are in the public domain. However, if selected and arranged creatively, the arrangement of those facts may be entitled to copyright protection as a compilation.

Sometimes similarity of expression may have to amount to verbatim copying or very close paraphrasing before the copyright of a factual work is infringed. Instructions and recipes fall into this category, although, if explanations or directions accompany them, there may be a basis for copyright protection.

Because copyright does not protect an author's labor, according to the Supreme Court, a subsequent author may build on a prior author's ideas and theories without wasted effort. For example, when A. A. Hoehling sued Universal City Studios for basing a movie on a theory revealed in his book on the mysterious destruction of the German dirigible *Hindenberg*, the court held that the sabotage hypothesis espoused in his book was based entirely on the interpretation of historical facts and was not copyrightable. *Hoehling v. Universal City Studios, Inc.*, 618 F.2d 972 (2d Cir. 1980).

Fact compilations—including directories, indexes, and maps—are works formed by collecting and assembling preexisting data. The copyrightability of factual compilations depends on the amount of skill and discretion used in arranging and selecting the underlying data. The art lies in the editing, the personal taste, and the clever arrangement of material. If a fact compilation lacks the requisite degree of creativity (e.g., a simple A-to-Z listing of telephone numbers for a city or town), even verbatim copying of large amounts of public domain data from the compilation is not copyright infringement (see Chapter 5, "What Copyright Doesn't Protect").

> **TIP** Generally, mere facts or ideas (separate from their expression) found in nonfiction works such as histories, biographies, investigative reports, exposés, and social and political commentaries can be paraphrased, provided you do not closely follow the overall structure of the work. However, be aware that for copyright purposes, close paraphrasing can be the same as copying. The closer you come to the original, the closer you are to infringing someone's copyright.

2.17.2.3   Fiction and Creative Nonfiction

Unlike fact-based works, fictional works, which may be expressed in an infinite number of ways, enjoy broad protection. You do not have to show verbatim copying or even close paraphrasing to prove copyright infringement.

However, where the similarities relate solely to standard elements derived from a common theme, or a common pool of literary techniques, there can be no infringement. These standard devices are analogous to unprotected ideas. At most, similarities in general ideas and common themes show that there is rarely anything new under the sun. Thus, an author's exclusive rights are largely confined to the details of his or her presentation. As one federal court judge stated, "The essence of infringement lies in taking not a general theme but its particular expression through similarities of treatment, details, scenes, events and characterizations."

In evaluating whether an entire work has been infringed, the proper question a judge or jury must ask is whether the defendant captured the *total concept and feel* of the original work. If the answer is yes, and what was copied was sufficiently original, copyright infringement probably exists. Highly original expression, even in a nonfiction account, enjoys a high degree of protection. For example, if you closely paraphrase a creative nonfiction work it can constitute copyright infringement if the paraphrasing is extensive enough.

2.17.2.4 Visual Works

Visual works receive broad protection under copyright law because of the endless ways in which they can be expressed. Because there are so many options available, there is no real danger in extending an author's monopoly over the ideas contained in a visual work. Again, the key to determining whether an infringement has occurred is whether the defendant has captured the total concept and feel of the original. While the isolated elements that make up a work of art may be uncopyrightable, the unique combination of those elements, or overall design, may be entitled to protection.

2.17.2.5 Audiovisual Works

Where there is a change in format (e.g., a TV series based on a motion picture or book), courts look at the total concept and feel of the two works, not minute differences, to determine whether there has been an impermissible amount of copying. The standard test involves comparing the expressive elements of the works (i.e., theme, mood, pacing, setting, characterization, and sequence of events). As a rule, copyright infringement will be considered to exist only if the defendant goes beyond copying vague plot outlines and actually appropriates concrete details or the fundamental essence and structure of the work.

2.17.3   What Are the Defenses to Copyright Infringement?

The most common defenses to copyright infringement are:

1. Fair use
2. Independent creation, without reference or access to the other work (Remember the scene in *Close Encounters of the Third Kind* in which people across the country, unbeknownst to each other, were seen making sculptures of the alien landing site? Assuming for the moment that mashed-potato sculptures are copyrightable works, that was *not* copyright infringement.)
3. Use of public domain (i.e., unprotected) materials

4. Authorized use, either granted expressly or impliedly
5. Inexcusable delay in filing a complaint despite knowledge of the infringement
6. The statute of limitations (three years from the moment the infringement could reasonably have been detected)

Refer to Chapters 3 and 4 for more information about the fair use and public domain defenses to copyright infringement.

2.17.4   Is Ignorance a Proper Defense to Copyright Infringement?

When Mark Twain was alerted that he had inadvertently cribbed the dedication to *The Innocents Abroad* from a book of poems by Oliver Wendell Holmes, he quipped, "Adam was the only man who, when he said a good thing, knew that nobody had said it before him." What Mark Twain did not realize is that under copyright law, ignorance (or innocent intent) is not bliss. As a matter of law, a plaintiff does not have to prove any knowledge or intent by the defendant to prove copyright infringement. Just ask George Harrison, whose song "My Sweet Lord" unconsciously infringed the Chiffons' 1963 hit, "He's So Fine." Anyone who violates any of the exclusive rights of a copyright owner—consciously or unconsciously—is an infringer. Of course, bad-faith infringers are treated more harshly than innocent ones when monetary damages are awarded.

2.17.5   What Are the Penalties for Copyright Infringement?

If you are thinking of copying without permission, think again. There are serious civil and criminal penalties for copyright infringement. The arsenal of civil remedies for copyright infringement includes monetary damages (i.e., actual damages, the infringer's profits, or statutory damages of up to $100,000 per infringement where *willfulness* exists), attorneys' fees, injunctions, impoundments, and destruction of infringing copies.

The Copyright Act entitles a plaintiff to elect to recover statutory damages instead of actual damages. Statutory damages exist because it is often hard to prove actual damages or profits. Statutory damages range from a minimum of $500 to a maximum of $20,000 per work infringed. However, if a copyright owner can prove that the infringement was willful, the damages can be as high as $100,000. The actual amount of the award is within the discretion of the court. If the infringer acted innocently, damages can be as low as $200. In addition, a judge, at his or her discretion, may reimburse costs, including attorneys' fees, to the prevailing party. The U.S. Attorney General also has within his or her power the ability to prosecute willful copyright infringers.

While it is true that most infringement actions wind up being settled, the settlement sums, inclusive of attorneys' fees, almost always exceed what a proper license would have cost in the first instance. In 1994, *New York Newsday* was sued for digitally altering two photographs—without permission—for a cover story on the infamous Tonya Harding–Nancy Kerrigan incident. Reportedly, the newspaper settled the case for $20,000—a sum approximately ten times what *Newsday* would have paid for a legitimate license.

3

Fair Use

[Fair use] distinguishes between a true scholar and a
chiseler who infringes a work for personal profit.
> *Wainwright Securities, Inc. v. Wall Street Transcripts Corp.*,
> 558 F.2d 91 (2d Cir. 1977)

Fair use is a privilege. It permits authors, scholars, researchers, and educators to borrow small portions of a copyrighted work for socially productive purposes without asking permission or paying a fee. Fair use (which is technically a defense to copyright infringement) acknowledges that copyright is not an absolute right. The purpose of the *fair use doctrine* is to avoid rigid application of the copyright laws in ways that might stifle the growth of knowledge, as the growth of knowledge is the ultimate goal of copyright.

Without fair use, a book reviewer couldn't quote excerpts from a new book in a critical review, and a historian couldn't quote a passage from a prior work to illustrate his or her observations without being guilty of copyright infringement. Unfortunately, there are no mathematical formulas to help you determine with certainty whether a particular use is a fair use. Only a court can do that. Nonetheless, there are guidelines that can help you, or your attorney, make these sometimes risky judgment calls.

3.1   What Kinds of Uses Are Usually Fair Uses?

To qualify as fair use, the use itself must first be for a protected use. Following are the kinds of protected uses that often qualify as fair uses:

- Criticism or parody (e.g., a quote in a review for purposes of illustration or comment, or a parody of an original work)

- News reporting (e.g., a summary of an address or article, with brief quotes, in a news article)
- Classroom teaching (e.g., reproducing a small part of a work to illustrate a lesson)
- Scholarship and research (e.g., a quote of a brief passage in a scholarly or technical work, for illustration or clarification of the author's observations)

CAUTION None of these uses is automatically considered a fair use. You should consider all of the circumstances and general limitations discussed in this chapter in weighing whether a particular use is fair or foul.

3.2   How Much Can You Borrow for Fair Use Purposes?

Fair use is impossible to quantify. One way of looking at fair use is to think of it as implied permission for reasonable use of another author's work. It is often helpful to ask yourself, "If someone borrowed x number of words from me without asking my permission, would I believe the use was fair?" If the answer is no, it's time to think about asking for permission. Confucius said it best: "What you do not want done to yourself, do not do to others." One well-known trade-book publisher advises its authors to obtain permission whenever text quotations exceed 250 words or more from a single full-length book. Many publishers use 300 words as the benchmark for fair use. This applies to either a single quote of 300 words or several shorter quotes that cumulatively equal 300 words.

According to a leading college-textbook publisher, no more than two lines of a poem (or song lyric), no matter how long the original work is, should be reprinted without consent. By contrast, John Wiley & Sons requires permission for *any* portion of a poem or song used by its authors. As you can see, these guidelines are merely publishers' rules of thumb, not enforceable legal definitions. The particular facts of a given case would determine whether these guidelines would hold up in court.

TIP Some publishers include a statement on the copyright page noting that short excerpts up to a specified word count may be reprinted in critical reviews or articles relating to the work without further permission. In such instances, the publishers have defined what they consider fair use, and no further permission is required for the specified excerpts.

3.3   A Four-Factor Test for Determining Fair Use

Unfortunately, there are no magic numbers of words, frames, or musical notes you can safely use without permission. Moreover, you cannot ensure fair use simply by using quotation marks and acknowledging the author of the borrowed material. Only a court can authoritatively determine whether a particular use is a fair use.

Based on the particular facts of a given case, courts consider the following four factors found in the Copyright Act to determine whether a particular use is fair:

1. The purpose of the use, including whether the use is primarily for commercial or noncommercial purposes
2. The nature of the work
3. The amount and the importance of the portions used, in relation to the whole of the original work
4. The effect of the new use on the potential market for, or value of, the original

Because fair use is an instinctive test, these four factors are not the only ones a court may consider.

TIP   While no single fair use factor is decisive, recent court decisions consider the fourth factor—the impact on the market for the original work—the most important.

3.3.1   Factor 1: How the Copyrighted Work Is Being Used

Courts typically consider three subfactors when examining how a work was used: (1) whether the use was socially productive; (2) whether the use was commercial or noncommercial; and (3) whether the user acted in good faith.

3.3.1.1   Socially Productive Uses

This subfactor asks whether the new work replaces the original, or whether it adds something new, thereby transforming the original work with new expression, meaning, or message. In copyright jargon, this is called a "transformative" use. The more transformative the new use, the more leeway the new use is given. This is because transformative works, which benefit the public, are more likely to further the goals of the Copyright Act (i.e., the progress of art and science).

Transformative uses add benefit to the public beyond the first author's work. Examples of transformative uses include (1) brief quotations in a scholarly or technical work to explain the author's observations; (2) parody, where the original work is the object of the parody; (3) a news report that summarizes a speech or article using brief quotations; and (4) a short quote in a book review that illustrates the reviewer's point of view.

CASE AND COMMENT

In *Campbell v. Acuff-Rose Music, Inc.*, 114 S.Ct 1164 (1994), 2 Live Crew, a well-known antiestablishment rap group, wrote new lyrics to Roy Orbison's classic rock song, "Oh, Pretty Woman." Because the new song, a parody entitled "Oh, Hairy Woman," commented on the banal values epitomized in the original song and did not compete with the original, the Supreme Court held that the use was a transformative use, which, although commercial in nature, was within the bounds of fair use.

Writing in a popular style does not remove the work from the scope of fair use. While courts sometimes make subjective judgments about the quality of a work (highbrow is good; lowbrow is bad), the key is whether, and to what extent, the new work comments on the copyrighted work itself. If the new work is not transformative, the use probably isn't fair.

3.3.1.2 Commercial Use

The second subfactor asks whether the motive for using the original work is to avoid paying a fee, or to avoid creating something independently. Nonprofit educational purposes are favored over for-profit ventures, although a profit motive, in and of itself, will not short-circuit a fair use defense. However, if the user stands to profit from using the copyrighted material without paying the usual fee, the use is suspect in the eyes of the law. For example, in *Original Appalachian Artworks, Inc. v. Topps Chewing Gum, Inc.*, 642 F. Supp. 1031 (N.D. Ga., 1986), a federal district court in Georgia refused to find fair use for Garbage Pail Kids sticker cards featuring off-color spoofs of the then-popular Cabbage Patch Kids dolls. In the court's view, the aims of the stickers "were merely to capitalize on the Cabbage Patch Craze".

On the other hand, even though an author or publisher has a profit motive, if the use is transformative—or falls into one of the enumerated fair use categories (i.e., criticism, comment, teaching, news reporting, scholarship, or research)—there is no automatic presumption that the use is unfair. Similarly, nonprofit educational users of copyrights should bear in mind that they are not automatically insulated from the law of copyright. It is the use, not the user, that determines fair use.

TIP 🖝	A work that merely repackages copyrighted material or that competes with the original is an unlikely candidate for fair use.

3.3.1.3   Bad Faith

Bad faith is the third subfactor used to determine whether a particular use meets the standards of fair use. If a work was improperly obtained, chances are the use will be disfavored. Errors or inaccuracies in copying the work also weigh against finding fair use. If you don't use quotation marks or you attempt to pass off someone else's work as your own, these factors will weigh against finding fair use, too.

For a long time, many attorneys felt that if you were denied permission but used the material anyway, it would be considered an act of bad faith. Recently, the U.S. Supreme Court held that being denied permission is immaterial if the use meets the standards of fair use. Nonetheless, many publishers insist on having permissions—even when a use is arguably fair— to avoid even the threat of litigation.

3.3.2   Factor 2: The Nature of the Copyrighted Work Used

The second factor focuses on two things: (1) the degree of creativity of the original copyrighted work, and (2) whether the original work was previously published. Not all copyrighted works are created equal. The doctrine of fair use is applied differently to different types of work. Therefore, the following may provide some guidance in analyzing the limits of fair use.

3.3.2.1   Creative Works versus Factual Works

The more creative a work, the more protection it receives against copying. Because of this, fiction and creative nonfiction receive greater protection than do works that have strong factual or functional elements. For instance, the front page of your morning newspaper receives less protection than the op-ed page, which creatively comments on the news of the day. As another example, a new account of the causes of World War I may report the same chronology of facts and repeat the same theories found in an earlier work, provided that the new work doesn't copy the truly expressive elements of the first work. A good rule of thumb is to never borrow more of a factual work than is necessary to get your point across. Protection of factual material may be thin, but it does exist.

3.3.2.2   Quotations

Using an excerpt or quote simply to display an author's colorful writing style (except, of course, in the context of literary criticism) is frowned on by the law. As a general rule, courts tolerate only modest copying of an author's colorful or original expression. The copyright laws are, after all, designed to protect an author's original means of expression. Of course, extemporaneous statements receive no copyright protection because they are not fixed in a tangible medium (see Chapter 2, "Copyright Basics").

If you do plan to quote a particular author's prose, make certain it is used to convey relevant facts or to paint a picture of his or her character. If it is used simply to enliven your text, you may be considered a chiseler, not a scholar. Even in a biography, you do not have a wholesale license to take the liveliest or most entertaining part of the subject's writings.

3.3.2.3   Pictures and Graphic Works

Pictorial and graphic works receive greater protection than text-based works because they are usually highly creative, as opposed to functional. Consequently, it is very difficult to make a fair use of such works, although there are limited scholarly, educational, news, and incidental use exceptions. Some elements of otherwise unprotectable pictorial and graphic works may still be protected by copyright. For instance, with respect to maps, while factual elements such as town names, geographic boundaries, and transportation routes are not protectable, the layer of art and text added to the basic map may be eligible for copyright.

Fair use of tables and graphs will depend on the amount of creativity employed in bringing together, organizing, and arranging previously existing information. As a general rule, garden-variety grids showing the relationships among common data, presented in a straightforward manner, are not copyrightable. However, graphic elements contained in the grid may be entitled to protection.

> **TIP**
>
> If you are trying to claim fair use of a visual work, be aware that it is harder to justify reproducing a work in full color than in black and white. Moreover, if your purpose is academic or scholarly, a thumbnail illustration lends itself better to fair use than does a full-page reproduction.

3.3.2.4   Scientific and Scholarly Works

Scientific works, when used for research or scholarly purposes, receive less protection than do nonscientific works. While there isn't limitless fair use in this area, courts are more liberal in their fair use analysis with such works because they do not want to discourage authors from dealing with important topics. If a particular theory is the focus of critical attention, the more transformative the use, the more the degree of permissible copying will increase.

3.3.2.5   Published versus Unpublished Works

The scope of fair use is narrower for unpublished works than for published works. Thus, red flags should go up when you intend to use an *unpublished* work without consent. While there is no rule prohibiting the use of unpublished materials, you stand a better chance of being sued if you quote from an unpublished work. Authors generally have the right to decide whether or when (and in what form) to first publish their works. Consequently, the fact that a work is unpublished weighs against finding the use fair. See Section 3.3.2.6 for the legal definition of the word *publication*.

CASE AND COMMENT

In *Harper & Row Publishers v. Nation Enterprises*, 471 U.S. 539 (1985), a case that went all the way to the U.S. Supreme Court, *The Nation* scooped *Time* magazine by publishing verbatim excerpts from a stolen copy of President Ford's unpublished memoirs. This caused *Time* to cancel its contractual commitment to publish prepublication excerpts from the book. While only 300 words from a 20,000-word manuscript were taken, the Supreme Court held that *The Nation* infringed Harper & Row's copyright.

The key factor against finding fair use was the unpublished nature of the work. Also, while quantitatively small, what The Nation *took was "essentially the heart" of the book. By taking more of the author's expression than was needed to illustrate a news story, and thereby scooping* Time, The Nation *destroyed the market for first serial rights. Had the quotations been used sparingly for a critical book review, the results might have been different. It is worth pointing out that the defendant in this case was a not-for-profit corporation.*

In response to the outcry of scholars and writers, Congress amended the Copyright Act in 1992 to make it clear that fair use is not automatically barred just because a work is unpublished. What this means is that while the unpublished nature of a work is still a very important factor weighing against fair use, it is not decisive.

Keep in mind that copyright ownership of letters, including e-mail, belongs to the author, not to the recipient. While the recipient owns the right to sell an unpublished letter, or to give it away, the recipient cannot, without permission, reproduce it or, in the case of e-mail, retransmit it.

3.3.2.6   *What Is the Legal Definition of the Word* Publication?

Publication requires authorized distribution of multiple copies of a work to the public by sale, rental, lease, or loan. Thus, anyone who photocopies or duplicates an existing work should be aware that personal letters or diaries on deposit with a library or research facility may be considered unpublished works. Donor or institutional restrictions—whether expressed or implied—on who can use the papers, and for what purposes, would suggest that the papers are unpublished. Similarly, libraries do not usually have the right to distribute personal papers for purposes of further distribution, another hallmark of publication. That authority resides with the copyright owner (or his or her estate), provided the work is still in copyright (see Chapter 4, "What's in the Public Domain?").

3.3.3   Factor 3: The Amount and Importance of the Material Used

The third fair use factor considers two things: (1) the amount of material copied, and (2) whether it was a key element of the copyrighted work. As a rule, a use is less likely to be considered fair whenever the portion of the original material used is relatively large or is a particularly powerful, interesting, or juicy part of the original work. Thus, using even a small portion of another's work may be an infringing use if what is taken is considered the heart of that work.

The extent of permissible copying varies with the purpose and character of the use. Quoting 50 words from a well-known politician's memoirs in the context of a critical review is probably okay. Using 50 words from a Maya Angelou poem in an anthology of contemporary American poets probably constitutes copyright infringement.

Under the fair use doctrine, an author is allowed to take just enough to ensure that readers understand what the author is criticizing or commenting on—nothing more. Where the object of the analysis is the copyrighted work itself, the scope of fair use expands. In an extreme case, one federal court held that fair use extended to a conservative group's reproduction of an entire ad from *Hustler* magazine in the group's antiobscenity fund-raising campaigns. Anything less than the entire repulsive message, the court reasoned, would have been inadequate to convey the group's statement about pornography and to refute a private attack on the group's leader, Reverend Jimmy Falwell. *Hustler Magazine, Inc. v. The Moral Majority, Inc.*, 796 F.2d 1148 (1986).

At the other extreme, the U.S. Supreme Court has held that 300 words taken from President Ford's unpublished memoirs was not fair use because it adversely affected the current and potential market for the work and it made off with the heart of the work. These two cases illustrate that there are no mechanical rules. However, you should assume that you should seek permission for anything more than limited use of copyrighted material. Thus, quote only as much as is absolutely necessary to get your point across. After all, most long quotes can be paraphrased.

3.3.4   Factor 4: The Effect on the Potential Market for the Copyrighted Work

The final fair use factor looks at the effect of the infringing use on the potential market for the original work. Here, the key concern is that the new use should not undercut the market for the work you are copying from. As mentioned previously, this factor is considered by many courts to be the most important fair use consideration.

Because licensing and the sales of subsidiary rights sometimes generate more revenue than the sale of the work in its original form, the potential market for a work includes much more than the sale of copies of the work itself; it also includes permission fees. Because publishers profit from the licensing of permissions (which publishers routinely split 50/50 with book authors), a use that deprives a publisher of a permission fee is relevant to the fair use analysis. However, if the use only slightly impairs the current or potential market for the work, this minor harm to the potential market for the work will not necessarily scuttle a fair use defense.

3.3.4.1   Criticism, Unflattering and Otherwise

Bona fide criticism is usually a fair use because copyright holders do not license book, movie, or theater reviews. Therefore, even a bad review that kills sales of the original copyrighted work is not relevant to the fair use analysis. Nonetheless, you cannot—under the pretense of a review—publish so much of the original that it is unnecessary for the public to purchase the original work.

3.3.4.2   Out-of-Print Works

Because there is little reason to expect future harm to a work that is no longer commercially available, courts sometimes give users of out-of-print works some leeway. This, however, does not mean that it is proper to use an out-of-print work without permission; fair use depends on application of *all* the fair use factors.

Moreover, in the current digital environment, where copying of chapter-length excerpts from books is cheap and easy, the fact that a work is currently out of print is becoming irrelevant. The digital storage of information as bits and the demise of static media as the format of choice for long-shelf-life nonfiction mean that books never have to go out of print. Thus, unless there is an unambiguous statement that a work won't be reissued or republished in any form, you can no longer rely on a work's out-of-print status to suggest fair use.

3.4   Special Fair Use Situations

Most fair use cases are decided on the four primary fair use factors. However, there are a couple of special uses that require more analysis: (1) parody, the most troublesome fair use issue of all, and (2) educational uses.

3.4.1   What about Parody and Satire?

Parody is a unique form of criticism or comment that pokes fun at the original to make a point. However, unlike literary criticism, parody is not usually presumed to involve fair use, chiefly because parody liberally borrows from the work being satirized, and it is usually produced for profit. Because copyright owners turn purple when their works are ridiculed, it is easy to see why parody is often a flash point for litigation.

Ultimately, parody is judged fair or foul based on an analysis of the four fair use factors. However, because hardly any parody is done for noncommercial purposes, and few copyright holders are willing to grant licenses to parodists, the courts treat parody differently from other potential fair use situations. Keep in mind, too, that judges sometimes impose their own tastes on the public. While good clean fun is all right, risqué humor or sexual innuendo often is not. For example, in MCA, Inc. v. Wilson, 677 F.2d 180 (1981), a federal court of appeals saw no humor in a defendant's risqué send-up, full of sexual connotations and innuendoes, of the Andrews Sisters' 1940s recording of "Boogie Woogie Bugle Boy."

As a general rule, parodists are allowed to conjure up the original work (and sometimes even use a substantial portion to evoke recognition), provided it comments on the original author's work, and the parody is reasonably apparent. The greater its separate identity, the more leeway the parody will be given. The key is that the new work must comment on the original, altering it with new expression, meaning, or message. If there is no awareness of the original, it is probably piracy, not parody. As a general rule, you cannot satirize an unknown work. Similarly, while a parody does not have to succeed to be protected by fair use, if the audience doesn't get the joke, it may be labeled a rip-off, not ridicule. Therefore, if the parody is not clearly recognizable, labeling the work may help, although there is neither a rule requiring that you do so nor a guarantee that doing so will shield you from liability.

CAUTION Under federal and state trademark dilution laws, a parody of a famous trademark—which includes well-known characters, designs, shapes, symbols, and slogans—may expose you to the risk of being sued. Under federal law, the owner of a famous mark can stop the commercial use of the mark if that use diminishes the distinctive quality of the trademark. While there are exceptions for fair use in competitive advertising, noncommercial uses, and news reporting, as of this writing there is little case law to provide guidance. However, these exclusions should accommodate most First Amendment free speech concerns, provided you do not intend to trade on the owner's reputation or goodwill.

3.4.2   What about Fair Use by Educators?

While reproduction of copyrighted material in an academic or classroom environment is not the focus of this book, it is worth noting that nonprofit educational copiers can be held liable for copyright infringement if they go beyond limited, occasional copying and undermine copyright owners' rights, markets, or materials. That is, federal copyright law applies to educators and educational institutions also.

3.4.2.1   Are There Any Fair Use Guidelines for Educators?

While they are not the law, certain classroom guidelines for use of books and periodicals were endorsed by a 1976 House Committee Report covering educational copying. The guidelines set minimum, not maximum, standards of educational fair use. The guidelines allow (1) copying that meets the test of brevity (e.g., a complete article, story, or essay of less than 2,500 words; or an excerpt from a lengthy prose work, duplicating up to at least 500 words, extending to 1,000 words or 10 percent of the work, whichever is less; one chart, graph, diagram, drawing, or picture per book or periodical); (2) copying that meets the test of spontaneity, under which "the inspiration and decision to use the work and the moment of its use for maximum teaching effectiveness are so close in time that it would be unreasonable to expect a timely reply to a request for permission"; (3) no more than nine instances of multiple copying for one course during one class term, and only limited copying from any single author or collective work; (4) the inclusion of a copyright notice on each copy; (5) the assurance that copying does not "substitute for the purchase of books, publishers' reprints or periodicals"; and (6) the provision that no student is charged more than the actual cost of the photocopying, if any fee is charged at all.

For more information, write to the Copyright Office, Library of Congress, Washington, DC 20559, and request Circular 21, "Reproduction of Copyrighted Works by Educators and Librarians." You can also visit the Stanford University Library website at www.fairuse.stanford.edu/library, which contains additional copyright guidelines for educators and students.

3.4.2.2   Copyright Clearance Center (CCC)

If a contemplated academic use exceeds the boundaries of fair use, the Copyright Clearance Center (CCC) (www.copyright.com), a permissions agent, provides a convenient mechanism for the licensing of academic course packets and classroom handouts. The CCC can be contacted at 222 Rosewood Drive, Danvers, MA 01923, 508-750-8400.

3.5   Real-Life Examples of Fair Use

The following are brief summaries of real-life examples of uses declared fair by courts. Keep in mind that criticism, news reporting, scholarship, research, and teaching are only *potential* fair uses. Fair use requires a delicate balancing of all four fair use factors discussed earlier in this chapter. If there is any doubt whether a proposed use is fair, obtain permission or seek legal advice.

Time, Inc. v. Bernard Geis Associates, 293 F. Supp. 130 (S.D.N.Y. 1968).   The court held that charcoal drawings of a plaintiff's home movie of the Kennedy assassination, used to illustrate a conspiracy-theory book, was a fair use. The court found that the serious nature of the book, the public's interest in information about the assassination, and the fact that Time, Inc., suffered little economic injury favored fair use.

Maxtone-Graham v. Burtchaell, 803 F.2d 1253 (2d Cir. 1986).   An appellate court held that the verbatim copying of interviews amounting to 7,000 words (4.3 percent) from an out-of-print pro-choice book, by the author of an antiabortion book critical of the first book, was a fair use. The court reasoned that fair use favors criticism and commentary, especially when competition between the works does not exist.

Narell v. Freeman, 872 F.2d 907 (9th Cir. 1989).   An author's use of factual material from a nonfiction book, to provide context for her historical novel, was ruled permissible because the scope of fair use is greater with informative works than with creative works. The court held that taking a few ordinary phrases and mostly factual statements to create a non-competitive work was within the bounds of fair use.

New Era Publications International, ApS v. Carol Publishing Group, 904 F.2d 152 (2d Cir. 1990).   On appeal, an appellate court held that the use of quotations in an unflattering biography of Church of Scientology founder L. Ron Hubbard was a fair use. The court ruled that fair use favors critical biographies and that, on balance, the quoted material was more factual than expressive and thus was entitled to less protection. The court added that borrowing from published works was not unfair, especially where quotes were used to point out inconsistencies in official records and in the subject's alleged character defects. The court also held that any harm to sales of an authorized biography was irrelevant for copyright purposes because criticism, by definition, diminishes sales.

Mathieson v. Associated Press, 23 U.S.P.Q.2d 1685 (S.D.N.Y. 1992).   A non-profit news organization's unauthorized use of photos of Oliver North from a newsworthy sales brochure for body armor to accompany a related news article was deemed a fair use. The federal district court held that the use of photos of public figures for news reporting strongly favors fair use.

Norse v. Henry Holt and Co., 847 F. Supp. 142 (N.D. Cal. 1994).   The author of *unpublished* letters brought a copyright infringement action against the author and publisher of a biography of William S. Burroughs. The court held that copying 50 words from the unpublished letters in a scholarly work about a well-known literary figure was a fair use. Moreover, the defendants neither scooped the plaintiff nor published the heart of the plaintiff's work. On balance, the court determined that only one factor, the unpublished nature of the letters, favored the plaintiff.

3.6   Real-Life Examples of Foul Use

Here are some examples of infringing uses. Bear in mind that there is no general applicable definition of fair use, so each case must be decided on its own merits. Unfortunately, the reported cases sometimes seem to be in hopeless conflict with each other.

Harper & Row, Pubs, Inc. v. Nation Enter., 471 U.S. 539 (1985).   The U.S. Supreme Court held that the fair use news-reporting exception did not apply when a magazine quoted 300 out of 20,000 words that made up the heart of Gerald Ford's unpublished memoirs. The magazine's attempt to scoop *Time*, and the unpublished nature of the excerpt, plus the damage to the prepublication serialization, were all critical to the Court's analysis.

Salinger v. Random House, Inc., 811 F.2d 90 (2d Cir. 1987).   The court held that the use of verbatim quotes taken from one third of 17 unpublished J. D. Salinger letters and from 10 percent of 42 other works, for an unauthorized biography, was not a fair use. The court frowned on the fact that the "vividness" of the quoted materials was to "a large extent . . . [what] made [the] book worth reading," thereby displacing a market for the letters.

Lish v. Harper's Magazine Found., 807 F. Supp. 1090 (S.D.N.Y. 1992). A New York federal district court rejected a nonprofit magazine's fair use defense when it published 52 percent of a well-known editor's *unpublished* letter to students enrolled in his fiction-writing workshop. While there was no economic harm, the court determined that the magazine took more of Lish's protected expression than it needed to report a news story. The court also held that restricted distribution of the letter to 48 students was not publication, and that the defendant's nonprofit status did not bar liability.

Twin Peaks Productions, Inc. v. Publications International, Ltd., 996 F.2d 1366 (2d Cir. 1993). A publisher's fan book, which used 89 lines of dialogue from a popular TV series, plus detailed plot summaries of episodes, was held not to be a fair use. The court held that the plot summaries went beyond merely identifying plots for purposes of comment or criticism. What the defendant did was to abridge plots, creating an unauthorized derivative work, thus harming the market for official tie-in books.

Robinson v. Random House, Inc., 877 F. Supp. 830 (S.D.N.Y. 1995). The court rejected a fair use defense when 25 to 30 percent of a book on Pan Am's founder quoted or closely paraphrased a competing book. The court held that the author's expression of historical facts was protected by the Copyright Act. The court issued a permanent injunction prohibiting further distribution of the competing book without the plaintiff's permission.

CHECKLIST: **Fair Use**

☐ Fair use is not a simple test, but a delicate balancing of interests. Sometimes even a small (but important) portion borrowed from a larger work may constitute copyright infringement.

☐ While fair use favors criticism, comment, news reporting, teaching, scholarship, and research, these uses are *not* automatically deemed fair uses. Only a court can determine with authority whether a particular use is a fair use.

☐ Quoting from unpublished materials exposes you to greater risk than quoting from published materials. Although unpublished materials are not barred from fair use, their unpublished status weighs against fair use.

☐ Fact-based works, which can be expressed in limited ways, receive less copyright protection than fanciful works that can be expressed in multitudinous ways.

☐ Visual works enjoy a high degree of protection under copyright law.

☐ Synthesizing facts in your own words is more likely to be viewed as fair use than is verbatim copying. However, close paraphrasing may constitute copyright infringement if done extensively.

☐ Never copy more of a copyrighted work than is necessary to make your point understood. The more you borrow, the less likely it is that your use will be considered a fair use.

☐ Do not take the heart of the work you're copying from. If what you've copied is important to the original, it will weigh against finding fair use.

☐ Do not quote from a copyrighted work simply to enliven your own text. Make certain that you comment on the material you borrow or that you can otherwise justify its use.

☐ Never copy something to avoid paying permission fees or to avoid creating something on your own.

☐ Lack of credit, or improper credit, weighs against finding fair use. Nonetheless, providing author credit will not prevent you from being sued.

☐ Don't compete with the work you are quoting or copying from. If the use diminishes the market for the copyrighted work (or portions of it), including revenues from licensing fees, it is probably not a fair use.

4

What's in the Public Domain?

Copyright protection does not last forever—that's why copyright is often called a "limited monopoly." When copyrights grow old and die, the works they protect fall into the public domain. The term *public domain* (or "PD"), therefore, refers to works that are no longer protected by copyright. As we point out in Section 5.5, certain U.S. government works are automatically thrust into the public domain for policy reasons.

Knowing when a copyright expires will allow you to take advantage of the abundance of material found in the public domain. This requires a working knowledge of the old 1909 Copyright Act (effective through December 31, 1977), which we discuss in Section 4.2.1. The following is a sampling of works by well-known authors that entered the public domain on January 1, 1996, as reported by the editors of *The Public Domain Report Monthly*:

L. Frank Baum	*Glinda of Oz* (Illustrated by John R. Neill)
Irving Berlin	*Bells*
Anton Chekhov	*The Chorus Girl and Other Stories*
Noel Coward	*I'll Leave It to You*
T. S. Eliot	*Poems* (1920 edition)
F. Scott Fitzgerald	*Flappers and Philosophers*
Laura Lee Hope	*The Bobbsey Twins in the Great West*
D. H. Lawrence	*Women in Love*
Jack London	*Hearts of Three*
A. A. Milne	*Mr. Pim Passes By*
Edith Wharton	*The Age of Innocence*

4.1   If a Work Is in the Public Domain, Do You Have to Clear Rights?

Clearing rights to PD materials may sound like an odd concept, but other laws may protect a work long after its copyright has expired. In many cases, even if a work is in the public domain, rights to the material may be protected under various other legal theories, such as trademark or unfair competition laws (which protect a work against confusingly similar usage by another), an individual's right of privacy (the right to be left alone), or a person's right of publicity (an individual's exclusive right to profit from her or his name, voice, photograph, or likeness). New or later versions, to the extent the underlying PD work has been embellished with new material, may also require permissions.

4.1.1   How Do You Clear Rights to a Public Domain (PD) Work?

Whenever you rely on the PD status of a work, it is prudent to make sure that the particular version you wish to excerpt or reproduce is actually in the public domain. Any new expression—including editorial revisions, notes, illustrations, or other material added to an otherwise PD work—may be protected as a derivative work. Without obtaining the author's permission, you cannot use the fresh layer of material found in the new version of the old PD work.

Therefore, it's crucial that only the original PD version, not any later copyrighted versions, be used without permission. For example, *The Adventures of Pinocchio* (1883), by Carlo Collodi, the pen name of Carlo Lorenzini (1826–1890), is in the public domain. However, a new version (e.g., Disney's full-length animated classic) or an English-language translation of Collodi's story may be protected under copyright law as a derivative work—to the extent that new original material is added.

Bear in mind that a derivative work that passes into the public domain takes with it only the fresh new layer of material added to the earlier work. If the underlying work is still protected by copyright, that protection remains intact. Similarly, the copyright in a PD work is not revived even if the work is later adapted as a derivative work (see Chapter 2, "Copyright Basics").

Another consideration in approaching PD works is foreign copyright protection. While a work may be in the public domain in the United States, as discussed later in this chapter, it may still be protected outside the United

States by foreign laws, which require permissions for use in foreign territories (see Section 4.2.3, "What about Foreign Copyright Duration?").

Never assume that a work is in the public domain simply because you have access to that work on the Internet. Many works posted to the Internet have been posted without the copyright owner's consent.

While the following sections do not provide an exhaustive list, they do offer some basic guidelines for using specific types of PD materials. Remember, however, these guidelines are not a substitute for consulting with an attorney.

4.1.1.1   Using PD Literature

Later editions of PD works may contain enough new original material (e.g., preface, revision, and translation) to warrant separate copyright protection as a derivative work, thus requiring permissions. For example, although Susie Hoch's translation of Sigmund Freud's *A General Introduction to Psychoanalysis* fell into the public domain on January 1, 1996, a later translation of Freud's original work may still be protected by copyright.

Particular care is also needed when dealing with a work for which the copyright has expired for failure to renew under the Copyright Act of 1909. While the copyright in the main work may have expired, hidden under the surface are rights that may have to be cleared, including those for photos, excerpts from other copyrighted works, translation rights, and so on.

4.1.1.2   Using PD Art

Sometimes, PD artwork, particularly work illustrating distinctive characters (e.g., Beatrix Potter's *Peter Rabbit* illustrations), can achieve protection under trademark law and can function as a logo or a source identifier. Moreover, if the artwork depicts identifiable persons, trademarks, or products, obtaining rights from the persons identified or from the trademark owners may also be necessary if the work is used for commercial purposes, such as in an advertisement or for bed sheets. Recent cases also suggest that the particular style of an artist may be protected under trademark or unfair competition law.

Because photos of PD works may also be copyrighted, permission from the photographer, or the source of that photo, may also be required. This is often the case with photos of fine art, where there is sometimes no other way to get reproducible art, except from the source (e.g., a museum or gallery). While a photographer cannot claim copyright in a Renaissance masterpiece, reproductive photographs are, arguably, copyrighted works in their own right because of the aesthetic and technical judgments made by the photographer in capturing the underlying image.

4.1.1.3   Using PD Audiovisual Works

When copyright in a film, or other audiovisual work, falls into the public domain for nonrenewal, or for another reason, the elements of the film that are based on preexisting matter may still be protected under copyright. Therefore, multimedia and online publishers, whose works include sound and video, must be careful when working with audiovisual works. For example, in *Russell v. Price*, 612 F.2d 1123 (9th Cir. 1979), copyright in the film *Pygmalion*—based on George Bernard Shaw's play—was not renewed and fell into the public domain. However, Shaw's estate, which owned the copyright in the stage play on which the film was based, was able to prevent distribution and exhibition of the PD film. At the time, anyone who used the PD film would have infringed the copyright in Shaw's underlying play. Similarly, in 1974, the copyright for *It's A Wonderful Life*, the classic Frank Capra film starring Jimmy Stewart, fell into the public domain for failure to renew during the 28th year of publication. However, in 1993, Republic Pictures Home Video recaptured the copyright by purchasing the rights to the film score and underlying story, "The Greatest Gift," by Philip Van Doren Stern. Since the film score and the underlying story were still protected by copyright, the film could now be protected.

Most states also recognize an individual's right of publicity, the right to profit from his or her own celebrity (see Chapter 11, "Basics of Publicity and Privacy"). Accordingly, despite a film's PD status, actors and other performers (including stunt doubles, voice-over actors, etc.) may be entitled to reuse fees for their on-screen performances (see Chapter 8, "Multimedia Clearances"). Similarly, titles and characters may be protected as valid trademarks. Unlike copyrights, trademarks can live forever and enjoy broad protection. Also, props (including set dressings and wardrobe) and artwork (including sculptures) may require clearances if they figure prominently in a work, including a multimedia production, or if they have independent trademark significance (see Chapter 5, "What Copyright Doesn't Protect").

4.1.1.4   Using PD Music and Audio

More and more books are being adapted for multimedia or packaged with interactive software. Similarly, many websites feature text, images, and sounds. Website developers, in particular, should be aware that many separate copyrightable elements may be contained in a single music or audio clip, including lyrics, melodies, and so on. When copyright protection for a particular song ends, only the original version of the song passes into the public domain.

Later sound recordings—and different arrangements—may therefore be protected by copyright (besides copyright in the musical composition, there is a separate copyright in the sound recording). Thus, a special license may be needed from the owner of the sound recording if you want to reproduce a recording of a PD composition. Union reuse fees for the performances (including spoken words) embodied in a sound recording may also be needed to commercially exploit a particular recording of a PD song. If spoken words are involved, contact one of the performing arts guilds listed in Appendix E (SAG or AFTRA). As we have mentioned, the right of publicity protects a person's voice and his or her physical likeness.

One final note: The scope of fair use for recorded music is limited, and the "eight-bar rule" that you might have heard of is not the law; it's what some have called folklore. If you are contemplating using a piece of music, depending on the usage, you may need to clear rights with the music publisher (if it's still in copyright), the record company, and the performers.

4.1.2   What Are Some Resources for Locating PD Materials?

Here are some helpful guides for locating PD materials:

> The Mini-Encyclopedia of Public Domain Songs, BZ/Rights & Permissions, Inc., 125 West 72nd Street, New York, NY 10023, 212-580-0615
>
> The Public Domain Report Monthly, P.O. Box 3102, Margate, NJ 08402, 800-827-9401
>
> Information U.S.A. by Lesko, Matthew. (Penguin)—A comprehensive guide to what is free from the U.S. government, including a treasure trove of PD photographs, prints, and other materials

Other sources of PD material include corporate public relations departments and U.S. government agencies. One of the best sources of PD material is in the Library of Congress. For example, the library's Prints and Photographs Division (212-707-6394) has custody of more than 13 million prints, photographs, and drawings. However, do not assume that everything available from the U.S. government is in the public domain or is available for free. For example, Art Resource, a private rights and permissions agency, licenses the objects housed in The National Portrait Gallery, a division of the Smithsonian Institution, as well as other Smithsonian holdings.

4.2   How Long Does Copyright Protection Last?

The life expectancy of a copyright depends on the answers to the following four questions:

1. When was the work created?
2. Who created the work? (An individual? Two or more individuals? An employee?)
3. When did the author die?
4. When was the work registered or published?

4.2.1   Works Created before January 1, 1978

Works created before January 1, 1978, are protected under the old 1909 Copyright Act. Under the old act, works published or registered before January 1, 1978, may be protected for a total of 75 years, provided that certain copyright renewal formalities were followed.

4.2.1.1   Copyright Renewal Terms

As mentioned in Section 2.16, before January 1, 1978, the duration of all copyrights was split into two consecutive terms. Under the old law, copyright lasted only 28 years from the date the copyright was originally secured. However, the copyright was eligible for renewal during the last (28th) year of the initial term. If renewed in a timely manner, the copyright was extended an additional 28 years for a maximum of 56 years. In 1978, the second term was extended to 47 years, bringing the maximum period of copyright protection for pre-1978 works up to 75 years. Thus, a work that was originally copyrighted on September 11, 1930, had to be renewed during its 28th year, which was between September 11, 1957, and September 11, 1958. If not renewed by September 11, 1958, the work fell into the public domain.

In 1992, Congress amended the laws to make copyright renewal for pre-1978 works automatic. Before that date, if an author failed to renew within certain strict time limits, the work fell into the public domain, and all copyright protection was lost. For example, copyright protection for Frank Capra's classic film *It's a Wonderful Life* (1946) was lost in 1974 because someone inadvertently failed to file a copyright renewal application with the Copyright Office during the 28th year after the film's release or publication. Today, any copyright secured after January 1, 1964, is renewed automatically. Nonetheless, for copyrights secured prior to January 1, 1964, but not renewed on time, copyright protection expired at the end of their 28th calendar year, despite passage of the automatic copyright renewal law in 1992.

4.2.1.2   When Does the Copyright Clock Start Ticking?

Under the old 1909 Copyright Act, copyright was obtained either by publication (with proper copyright notice) or by registration as an unpublished work with the Copyright Office. As a general rule, if a work by an American author was published or registered more than 75 years ago, its copyright has expired. For purposes of computing the expiration of copyrights, since January 1, 1978, the law provides that all terms of copyright run through the end of the calendar year in which they would otherwise expire.

Generally, no permission or payment is needed to use a PD work. However, be careful not to confuse "out of print" with "out of copyright." "Out of print" is a temporary state that doesn't affect the copyright status of a work. "Out of copyright" is forever.

4.2.1.3   What Is Publication?

Under the old 1909 Copyright Act, a work was considered published (which started the copyright clock ticking) when it was either placed on sale or publicly distributed by the copyright owner or with the owner's permission. Restricted or limited distribution to a select group did not constitute "publication" under the old Copyright Act. Under current copyright law, which affects works created on or after January 1, 1978, the date an author dies, *not* the date a work is published, determines how long copyright protection endures. Unpublished works created on or *after* January 1, 1978, are automatically protected upon creation and endure for a term of 50 years after the author's death. For works for hire, anonymous works, and pseudonymous works created 1978 or later, copyright will last for 75 years from first publication or 100 years from creation, whichever is shorter.

4.2.1.4 How Long Does Copyright Last for Unpublished Letters, Diaries, Manuscripts, and Other Works?

Works created before January 1, 1978, but neither published nor registered for copyright are subject to special rules. Copyright in these works lasts for the life of the author plus 50 years (or 75/100 years in the case of works for hire), but in no case will their copyrights expire before December 31, 2002. Consequently, if you discover a new sonnet by William Shakespeare, or a Dead Sea scroll that's not been published, it is still copyright protected. Also, if the work is published before December 31, 2002, as a bonus, the term will be automatically extended another 25 years, until December 31, 2027.

For example, although Louisa May Alcott died in 1888, *The Inheritance*, a previously unpublished novel recently discovered by scholars in Harvard's Houghton Library, was still protected by copyright. Written when Alcott was just seventeen years old, it will remain protected until at least December 31, 2002, in its unpublished form. If the work is published before December 31, 2002, it will remain protected by copyright through the end of 2027.

> **Tip**   Copyrighted letters or other papers do not lose their unpublished status merely by placement in a library or other research facility if there are explicit or implicit restrictions concerning access or disclosure. For example, if you want to quote from Rachel Carson's unpublished letters, housed in the Beinecke Rare Books and Manuscript Library at Yale, you must obtain permission from Carson's literary executor and from the Beinecke Library. Carson's executor controls the copyright, while the library controls physical access. With few exceptions, a library cannot give you the legal right to publish material. What they can provide is access to material in their possession.

4.2.1.5 How Do You Determine Whether a Copyright Has Expired?

As mentioned previously, works published or registered before January 1, 1964, needed to be renewed by filing a copyright renewal registration in the 28th year following the original date of publication or registration. There are three ways to determine whether a copyright owner properly applied for a renewal copyright: (1) the Copyright Office can search its records for you for an hourly fee; (2) you can hire either a professional copyright search firm or a qualified attorney to do the same; or (3) you can search for it yourself, either in person or via Internet access to the Copyright Office files (see Appendix A, "How to Investigate the Copyright Status of a Work"). A good option is to use a professional search firm, which, besides understanding the idiosyncrasies of the copyright card system, will research nongovernmental entertainment and publishing databases to clarify the ownership of copyrights.

Bear in mind that the intricacies of researching copyright renewals, which contains many traps for the unwary, is beyond the scope of this book. However, a good starting point is *Researching Copyright Renewal: A Guide to Information and Procedure* (published by Fred B. Rothman) by Iris J. Wildman and Rhoda Carlson.

TIP   Copyrights obtained prior to January 1, 1964, had to be voluntarily renewed. If they were *not* voluntarily renewed on December 31st of their 28th year, they are now in the public domain.

4.2.2   Works Created on or after January 1, 1978

Works created on or after January 1, 1978, are protected under the 1976 Copyright Act. For practical purposes, you should assume that all works published on or after that date are protected by copyright and require permission. However, here is a quick overview of copyright duration for works created on or after that date. Copyrights created (fixed in a tangible medium) after December 31, 1977, are protected for the life of the author plus another 50 years. The earliest a 1978 copyright would expire is December 31, 2028, assuming, of course, that the author died in 1978.

If a work is prepared by two or more authors as a joint work, the copyright will expire 50 years after the death of the last surviving author.

Finally, copyright in works for hire, anonymous works, and works created under a pseudonym lasts for 75 years from first publication or 100 years from the date of creation—whichever is shorter.

4.2.3   What About Foreign Copyright Duration?

As we go to press, the rules concerning copyright duration in the United States differ significantly from those of many nations around the world. For example, most Western European authors enjoy a copyright term of life plus 70 years (for corporations the term is 70 years after they make the work available to the public). By comparison, U.S. authors enjoy a basic term of life plus 50 years (for pre-1978 works the maximum term is 75 years from either registration or publication).

Because many works will be exploited worldwide, a basic understanding of foreign copyright duration rules is important for permission requesters. This will allow you to calculate whether a work is in the public domain in a particular country. Of course, if a work is in copyright there, you cannot use that work (or any portion of it) in that country without first obtaining permission.

Unfortunately, there is no single body of international copyright law. Several treaties govern international copyright relations. The most important of these is the Berne Convention.

One key aspect of Berne is the principle of "national treatment." Under the national treatment rule, authors enjoy the same protection in other countries that those countries accord their own authors. For instance, a work by an Italian citizen is protected in the United States under our copyright laws. Similarly, a work by a U.S. author is protected in Italy under Italian copyright law.

However, there is an exception to the principle of national treatment known as "the rule of the shorter term." Under this rule, copyright for a foreign author in a Berne country *cannot* exceed the term the author enjoys in his or her own country. Because U.S. authors receive a scant life plus 50 years of protection in the United States, they receive 20 years less protection in Europe than their European colleagues.

Similarily, it is possible for a British work to expire in the United States before it expires in Great Britain. As a result, a U.S. publisher might be able to freely publish in the United States a British work that is in the public domain in the United States but not in Britain. For instance, James Joyce's *Ulysses* expired in 1997 in the United States but remains protected in Britain because British copyrights last for the life of the author plus an additional 70 years. If a publisher publishes, or adapts, *Ulysses* without the permission of Joyce's estate and sells it in Britain where they still protect the copyright, Joyce's estate can sue the publisher for copyright infringement.

Be aware also that certain foreign works that were previously in the public domain in the United States for failure to comply with certain technical requirements of our law (e.g., copyright notice) rose phoenixlike from the ashes on January 1, 1996. The United States restored these copyrights to life, and granted protection retroactively, because of the General Agreement on

Tariffs and Trade (GATT) negotiations. Eligible works were restored automatically. To be restored, these foreign works had to be copyright protected in their home country, but public domain in the United States.

CAUTION ⚠	As this is being written, legislation is pending in Congress to extend the copyright term in the United States an additional 20 years to bring it into conformity with the European Community.

TIP ☞	The term of protection for a work may expire in the United States before it expires in Europe or elsewhere. If there are foreign markets for your work, make sure you have cleared the underlying rights.

4.2.4   If a Work Is Missing Its Copyright Notice, Is It in the Public Domain?

Not necessarily. Once upon a time, if you failed to affix a proper copyright notice to your work (the familiar © followed by the publication date and the copyright owner's name), you risked total loss of copyright protection. In fact, many works now in the public domain are there because of inadvertent publication without notice or with improper notice. However, since March 1, 1989, copyright notice is no longer required. Further, if you're trolling the public domain looking for works to reuse, or republish, be aware that if notice was omitted in error on copies distributed between January 1, 1978, and March 1, 1989, copyright was not necessarily lost if certain corrective measures were taken to cure the oversight.

Copyright Duration and Renewal in Brief

Date of Copyright	Copyright Duration
Created 1978 or later	Author's life plus another 50 years; no renewal required.
Joint works created 1978 or later	50 years after the death of the last surviving author; no renewal required.
Anonymous works, pseudonymous works, and works for hire, created 1978 or later	75 years from publication, or 100 years from the year created, whichever comes first.
Published during 1964–1977	28 years from date of publication; 47-year renewal term is automatic for a total of 75 years; renewal is optional.
Published or registered prior to 1964, but less than 75 years ago	28-year initial term from date of publication or registration; 47-year renewal term if renewal registration filed in time, but if not, copyright has expired.
Created, but not published or copyrighted, prior to 1978	Life plus another 50 years, or a 75- or 100-year term. (If a work remains unpublished, copyright cannot expire prior to December 31, 2002. If a work is published by December 31, 2002, copyright cannot expire before December 31, 2027, no matter when the author died.)
Published more than 75 years ago	Copyright has expired in the United States.
Foreign copyrights	Governed by international treaties; work may be protected outside the United States, although PD in the United States; some foreign works formerly in the PD in the United States have been restored to copyright in the United States.

5

What Copyright Doesn't Protect

Certain works and subject matter—such as titles, names, short phrases, slogans, ideas, procedures, concepts, principles, and theories—are not protected under copyright law. As we discussed in Chapter 3, other works, while worthy of copyright protection, may be used for certain limited purposes without the copyright owner's permission if the use is a fair use. These exceptions and limitations give subsequent authors the necessary breathing space to build on prior authors' works without paying permission fees.

The following uses should be thought of as the public parks and utility rights-of-way of copyright law—narrow, but important, exceptions to the property interests of copyright owners. It is important to emphasize, however, that copyright protection is not the only legal protection for intellectual property. A work that isn't entitled to copyright protection may still be protected under some other legal theory (e.g., trademark law, contract law).

5.1   Ideas and Facts

Copyright protects only the way an author expresses an idea, not the idea itself. Ideas and other information revealed by an author's work are free for all to use without permission—so long as the author's particular form of expression isn't copied. For example, Jules Verne did not have a copyright on the *idea* of a science-fiction story, and CNN doesn't own the news that it reports, only the manner in which it is reported.

Generally, fact-based works—such as biographies, histories, and professional and technical works, where there are limited ways of expressing a particular idea—receive less protection than creative works such as novels, plays, and films, the ideas of which can be expressed in many ways. With

factual works, copyright protection may be so thin that only verbatim copying or close paraphrasing will count as infringement. Put another way, highly
expressive works (including creative nonfiction) are more likely to require
permission than are mostly factual ones.

However, it is important to remember that while copyright protection in
some factual material may be thin, it is not invisible. While the *facts* or
theories associated with a work may be in the public domain, the way an
author clarifies, vivifies, and interprets them may be entitled to copyright
protection. For example, if a writer, employing his or her literary license,
creates a hypothetical conversation between two historical figures, that
conversation will be copyright protected if it is clear from the context that
the conversation was not a verbatim report.

Moreover, while raw facts are not copyrightable, the creative way they are
arranged and assembled may be protected as a compilation copyright (see
Chapter 2, "Copyright Basics"). What a compilation copyright protects is the
arrangement itself, not the information within. Therefore, extracting pure
facts from a copyrighted work is not copyright infringement.

As a rule, the greater the universe of material from which to choose, the
more likely the compilation as a whole will be protectable. However, purely
functional arrangements (e.g., simple alphabetical listings of names, addresses,
and phone numbers in the "White Pages" phone books) that necessarily
follow in a particular sequence may be so mechanical as to be uncopyrightable,
notwithstanding the labor involved.

Unfortunately, no simple rule exists for distinguishing uncopyrightable
facts from their copyrightable expression. For example, where estimates or
appraisals are involved, courts are likely to treat the results as copyrightable
expression. In CCC *Information Services, Inc. v. Maclean Hunter Market Reports,
Inc.*, 44 F.3d 61 (2d Cir. 1994), an appellate court concluded that used-car
prices arranged by geographic areas, with adjustments for mileage and various options, were copyrightable because they represented editorial opinions,
not facts. In short, "soft" ideas, such as estimates that involve research and
creative interpretation of data, receive more protection under copyright law
than do mechanical averages.

5.2   Names, Titles, and Slogans

Names (including pen or stage names), titles, short phrases, and simple listings of ingredients are not copyrightable. This is because, in the opinions of
courts and the U.S. Copyright Office, these do not possess enough original
expression to warrant copyright protection.

Nonetheless, while names, titles, and slogans are not copyrightable, they may receive protection under trademark and unfair competition laws. Trademark law protects against consumer confusion and guards against the whittling away of the goodwill associated with a famous *mark* (shorthand for *trademark*), even when there is no confusion. Unfair competition law protects against "passing off" and "false designation of origin," which involve misrepresentations that might injure a person's business or personal reputation.

As a general rule, titles that are part of an ongoing series (e.g., "The Rough Guide," a series of travel destination guides) are protected under trademark and unfair competition law. Once a series title becomes identified in the public's mind with a particular publisher or other source, unfair competition law kicks in to protect against consumer confusion and predatory behavior.

Unlike series titles, which are strong trademark candidates, a title to a single work generally will not be protected under either trademark or unfair competition law, unless it is so widely used that it has become associated in the public's mind with a single source. Under trademark law, this mental association is known as "secondary meaning." Once secondary meaning has been established (generally, after long and exclusive use, strong sales, secondary use of the title on merchandise, significant advertising expenditures, and unsolicited media exposure), a single title may become a protected property right. That means if you plan to use a title that's become associated in the public's mind with some publisher or producer (whether it is the exact title or one confusingly similar), be prepared to ask for permission. Thus, calling your work "Gone with the Wind" may involve some risk, especially if the public is likely to assume that the estate of Margaret Mitchell granted permission for or sanctioned the new work.

5.3 Blank Forms and Standardized Materials

Because originality is the touchstone of copyright protection, blank forms (e.g., time cards, graph paper, account books, diaries, bank checks, scorecards, address books, report forms, order forms, etc., which are designed for recording information and do not in themselves convey information) are uncopyrightable. What constitutes a blank form, however, is sometimes hard to define. Similarly, solely informational works, such as height charts, standard calendars, and sporting schedules, which show an insignificant amount of creativity, are also uncopyrightable.

However, out of a sense of fairness, courts will try, where possible, to find copyrightable expression. While blank forms and standardized materials are not protectable, the manner in which they are arranged or coordinated, or the addition of copyrightable text or graphical designs, may be copyrightable.

5.4   Extemporaneous Speeches

Unprepared, extemporaneous speeches that are not recorded are not subject to copyright protection because they are not fixed in a tangible form. As we saw in Chapter 2, fixation is one of the three prerequisites for copyrightability. However, a speech may be protected if it is recorded simultaneously as it is being delivered, or if it is based on detailed notes or an original script. In such cases, the speech would be considered a protected derivative work (see Chapter 2, "Copyright Basics").

5.5   Government Works

A common misconception is that all works published by the government are in the public domain. In reality, only two kinds of government works may be used without permission: (1) United States government works created entirely by federal government employees as part of their official duties, and (2) certain works commissioned by the U.S. government as works for hire. In addition, some state and local works may be in the public domain.

5.5.1   United States Government Works

Ownership of materials created for the federal government by private-sector contractors is governed by contract law, not copyright law. If you plan to quote from a government publication, it is therefore advisable to write to the appropriate agency or department to see whether permission is required from the original contractor or grantee. Similarly, publication by the United States government of a copyrighted work does not throw that work into the public domain. This includes private copyrighted works prepared for or cited in federal government reports or documents. However, sparing use of this type of material might justify a fair use defense.

Works created by the United States Postal Service employees, however, are not free for the taking, because the U.S. Postal Service is not considered an agency of the United States government. This means that the Postal Service can use copyright law to prevent you from using its postage-stamp designs for T-shirts or other commercial purposes.

You may safely use transcripts of judicial opinions, administrative rules and laws, and related edicts, provided, of course, that they themselves don't quote from another copyrighted source. Although it is no longer mandatory to do so, when incorporating United States government works in your writings, you should identify the portion of your work for which you are claiming copyright protection as distinct from those portions consisting of U.S. government material. For example:

© Lloyd J. Jassin and Steven C. Schechter. Copyright claimed in entire work, exclusive of Appendixes A and B, which consist of official U.S. government publications.

Finally, the prohibition on copyright protection of United States government works does not apply to works by foreign governments, foreign government employees, or, for that matter, state governments.

5.5.2   State Government Works

Unlike federal government publications, state government works may be protected by copyright. However, as a matter of public policy, state and local court opinions, administrative rules and laws, and related edicts may be used without permission.

5.6   Standard Plots and Stock Characters

Dorothy Parker has been quoted as saying, "The only 'ism' Hollywood believes in is plagiarism." If a recently released Hollywood action-adventure movie, TV sitcom, or mystery novel seems vaguely familiar, you are probably right. All of them use highly conventionalized forms of expression to satisfy the public's need for something familiar. Artists borrow from, or pay homage to, artists who have preceded them. As a writer, you should not be ashamed to acknowledge this, provided you stay within the bounds of fair use.

Part of every novelist's, playwright's, and screenwriter's tool kit is a set of stock characters and scenes. Because copyright does not protect timeless literary themes, or the sequence of events that necessarily follows from them, stock scenes and conventional characters are exempt from copyright protection. The rationale for this is that certain highly conventional forms of expression, including stereotypical characters (the prostitute with the heart of gold), incidents (leading lady twists ankle, understudy takes over and saves the show), and plot devices (such as "good cop-bad cop" interplay), are basic, indispensable elements in the treatment given to certain specific topics. In the language of copyright law, these unprotectable forms of expression are known as "scènes à faire."

Two exceptions to the rule regarding conventional forms of expression apply to particular plots and distinctive characters.

5.6.1   Plots

While the prevailing view is that plots are not entitled to copyright protection, if a plot is sufficiently developed, it will be entitled to protection. For example, copyright will not protect the idea of a married socialite who coerces her lover to kill her husband for the insurance premium. Still, you can protect the plot idea as expressed in James M. Cain's novel *Double Indemnity* (or the 1944 Billy Wilder–Raymond Chandler screen adaptation).

As you move away from abstract plots and fill in the details—selecting a situation here, borrowing a character there, and then creating some connective fiber to hold it all together—authorship emerges, and copyright attaches. As Hollywood has shown time and again, it is permissible to reach into your writer's tool kit and rework the idea of someone who's taken to heaven ahead of schedule and returned to life in another man's/woman's/baby's/dog's body. What counts, for copyright purposes, is what is draped on the basic plot structure, not the structure itself.

5.6.2   Characters

Well-known characters, especially visually depicted ones, that are not merely stereotypes may be protected under copyright law, as well as under trademark and unfair competition laws. Courts, however, are split on whether literary characters can be protected by copyright outside the work in which they appear.

Nonetheless, even if a character is in the public domain, trademark and unfair competition law may protect the goodwill of a character if the character has gained commercial magnetism through public recognition. For example, Popeye, who made his first appearance in 1929 in a weekly cartoon strip called "Thimble Theatre," will slip into the public domain for copyright purposes on January 1, 2004. However, this does not preclude King Features, its owner, from claiming trademark rights in the character, or protecting later strips or nontrivial changes in the character. This would prevent you (1) from using the character, or the character's name, in any way that might imply that King Features sanctioned the use; or (2) from using it in a manner that tarnished the image of this famous trademark. Also, both later strips and nontrivial changes in the character will be protected as derivative works, to the extent that there is a fresh new layer of creative material present. Therefore, before using a well-known character, consult with an attorney, or consider asking for permission.

CHECKLIST: What Copyright Doesn't Protect

- ☐ You cannot copyright an idea, only the way in which the idea is expressed.
- ☐ You do not need permission to extract public domain information or raw facts from a copyrighted work because only an author's interpretation of facts is protected under copyright law.
- ☐ Numerical estimates and appraisals, based on judgment and expertise, may be protected as literary works.
- ☐ Titles, names, short phrases, slogans, familiar symbols and designs, and mere listings of ingredients (e.g., recipes) are not protected by copyright, but they may be protected under trademark and unfair competition law.
- ☐ If the title of a work has become broadly associated in the public's mind with a particular source, that title may be eligible for protection under trademark and unfair competition law.
- ☐ Blank forms such as invoice forms, designed solely to record information, are not copyrightable, although the addition of graphical elements and textual material (such as headings) may provide a basis for copyright protection.
- ☐ Truly extemporaneous speeches are not protected by copyright because they are not fixed in a tangible medium of expression—a prerequisite for copyright protection.
- ☐ U.S. government works, created entirely by federal government employees as part of their official duties, are in the public domain.

☐ Basic plot devices and standard settings are not entitled to copyright protection.

☐ Stock characters are not protected by copyright. However, well-
developed characters, especially visually depicted ones, may be
protected under both copyright and trademark laws.

6

Getting Permission

If your intended use is not considered a fair use, and the work you've drawn on is not in the public domain, you must obtain permission from the copyright owner for your intended use. Obtaining permissions and clearances is often a time-consuming, frustrating, and costly task. While permissions are sometimes obtained quickly and inexpensively, requested permissions are not always granted as quickly as expected—if they are granted at all. Therefore, you should always request permissions before your work is completed. Too often, permission requests are ignored, denied, or lost.

Ideally, the permission process should begin when you start researching and preparing your work. All sources of primary and secondary material should be flagged and identified using Form J in Appendix C. Knowing where a particular quote, passage, or photograph came from will save you hours of work later on. Direct quotes from previously published materials should be set off with quotation marks. For material in copyright, whether published or unpublished, having a citation will also ensure that the material is accurately reproduced and properly credited. Making sure you have the ability to verify facts and the accuracy of statements is also one of the best ways to avoid a libel claim (see Chapter 9, "Basics of Libel Law").

TIP Keep a log of all preexisting material you plan to use. For example, if you would like to use a particular photograph, make a note of the photo credit. Knowing that the photograph came from the National Archives can save you hours of valuable time and photo-research fees.

6.1 Who Is Responsible for Obtaining Clearances?

Generally, the responsibility for clearances—including the payment of license fees—falls on the author's shoulders, although some publishers may offer assistance or may agree to split the fee with you if there are many permissions. As a rule, publishers are very conservative when advising authors on seeking permission. As a courtesy to their authors, a few publishers may make permission arrangements on the authors' behalf, charging permission fees against future royalties. However, most authors and self-publishers who want to use copyrighted or other protected material—whether excerpts from a recent best-seller or lyrics to a popular song—will have to locate and negotiate with the owner of the material themselves.

TIP When negotiating your book contract, ask the publisher to provide a pool of funds, or a separate budget, for permissions and releases, or ask the publisher to split the cost with you. If the publisher agrees, you might ask to have these payments be nonrecoupable from future royalties. If the publisher insists on deducting the cost of permissions from future royalties, you might try to get the publisher to agree to waive repayment if the book doesn't earn royalties.

6.2 How Do You Determine Who the Copyright Owner Is?

Ownership of a copyright can be traced backward along certain basic ownership tracks. With the exception of a work for hire, which is described in this section and in Section 2.14, "Who Owns the Copyright to Work Made for Hire?" copyright vests automatically in the author at the time of creation. However, as we discussed in Chapter 2, nothing stops authors from selling, or assigning, their copyright interests.

If a work is a work for hire—that is, it is created on the job by an employee, or prepared pursuant to a written work for hire agreement—then the employer, or hiring party, not the creator of the work, is considered the author and copyright owner. Thus, if a freelancer creates a new work, but there is no prior written agreement, the freelancer, not the hiring party, is presumed to retain all rights in the copyright to that new work (see Chapter 7, "Dealing with Collaborators and Contributors").

6.3 Who Has the Authority to Grant Permission to Use a Split Copyright?

Often, permissions may be needed from more than one party. This is because each of the individual rights that make up a copyright can be subdivided (split up) and owned separately. For example, one person may control publication rights in the United States, while another may control publication rights abroad. Similarly, different parties may control the right to license the work for different activities, or in different media. In the case of derivative works and compilations, which contain layers of material contributed by different authors, it is imperative to determine all the holders of the rights in each of those layers of material. Accordingly, whenever requesting permission, always get the rights holders to confirm in writing that they own or control the copyright to the material. If they do not, you will need to obtain those additional rights from someone else.

6.4 How Do I Locate the Person Who Can Grant Me Permission?

There is no right or wrong way to go about locating the copyright owner, or the owner's authorized agent. However, the best place to start is with the formal copyright notice, or credit section, accompanying the work. The copyright notice is this familiar ©, followed by the year of first publication and the name of the copyright owner. While copyright notice is no longer required, fortunately, most works still contain one.

Obviously, the copyright notice identifies the copyright owner of the work at the time of publication. In many cases, the copyright owner listed in the work will be the current copyright owner, who can grant you the permission you need. If that person is no longer the copyright owner (which may be the case with older works that have changed hands many times over), he or she may be able to refer you to the right party. If the work has been registered with the Copyright Office, you can also trace the chain of ownership by conducting an "assignment search," which is discussed in Appendix A, "How to Investigate the Copyright Status of a Work."

Although you should always begin your search with the copyright notice, following are some time-saving tips for locating rights holders in specific kinds of works. In a pinch, your local reference librarian can also be extremely helpful.

6.4.1   Books

If you are excerpting a section from a book that is published in both hard-cover and paperback, write to the original hardcover publisher for permission, not the paperback publisher. Requests for permission should be sent to the publisher's permissions department. The publisher's address can be located on the copyright page, or in the *Literary Market Place* (LMP), published by R.R. Bowker. LMP is available from most libraries. Foreign publishers are listed in LMP's companion volume, *International Literary Market Place* (ILMP). If your library doesn't have a copy of LMP, it will probably have *Books In Print* (R.R. Bowker), which is a master guide to publishers, authors, and book titles. If the book is an older work, even though the publisher may no longer stock it, some, as a favor, will either provide a name of someone to contact or forward your request to the copyright owner.

If a publisher has gone out of business, or rights have reverted to the author, you might try to contact the Authors Registry (212-563-6920) (www.webcom.com/registry). The Registry, which distributes royalties for electronic uses of authors' works, maintains an "Authors Contact Directory." This database contains the names of thousands of authors, journalists, playwrights, poets, screenwriters, and literary agents. The Registry is an excellent resource, especially for locating freelance writers.

A few words of caution: If you are reprinting an introduction, bibliography, chart or graph, or any other supplemental material found in a book, ask the publisher whether the publisher also has the authority to grant permission to use that material. Be aware that split rights situations, discussed in Section 2.10, often apply in book publishing, so you may need to go to more than one source to get the rights you need. Also, if there are multiple editions of a work, make sure you are seeking permission from the copyright owner of the edition you are excerpting. Finally, if the author quotes from other sources in the passage you are reproducing, you may need permission from those original sources, too. Also remember that "out of print" does not mean "out of copyright."

6.4.2   Anthologies and Periodicals

Anthologies and periodicals are known as "collective works." Collective works have a dual copyright identity. Copyright in the overall work, which covers the selection and arrangement of existing contributions, is separate and distinct from copyright in the individual contributions. Examples of collective works include encyclopedias, newspapers, magazines, and other collections of existing works. Bear in mind that absent an agreement to the contrary, freelance writers and journalists usually grant only one-time print-publication rights to their publisher partners. However, there is a growing—and controversial—trend whereby freelance writers assign all rights to the publication. Thus, permission to use a particular contribution to a collective work generally must come from the author of the individual contribution, not from the publisher of the collective work. Of course, if a salaried writer prepares an article as part of his or her job, it will be considered a work for hire, and the publisher, not the writer, would be the proper party to grant permission (see Chapter 7, "Dealing with Collaborators and Contributors"). It is important to note that a newspaper or other periodical's right to grant permission does not extend to material provided by wire services, syndicates, and nonstaff writers and photographers.

Helpful resources include *Uhlrich's International Periodicals Directory* (R.R. Bowker), and the *Standard Periodicals Directory* (Oxbridge). To locate a particular author, or the author's representative, contact the Authors Registry (212-563-6920) (www.webcom.com/registry) or the Publication Rights Clearinghouse (PRC) (510-839-0110). The PRC is a collective licensing project of the National Writers Union, which clears electronic rights to periodical material.

6.4.3   Photographs, Charts, Figures, and Advertisements

Photographers—unless employed by a newspaper or other organization—often work as freelancers, or independent contractors. Thus, securing permission to use a photograph generally requires you to contact the photographer (or the photographer's representative) directly. If there is a credit line below (or beside) the image, it will tell you the name of the photographer (or photo agency) from whom the image was licensed. In addition to the photographer's copyright, other rights may be present. For example, a photograph may incorporate other copyrighted works, or it may depict a person, product, or place in a way that may expose you to legal liability for defamation, invasion of privacy, or trademark infringement. Depending on what intellectual property rights are present, and how the image is used, both a copyright permission and a model release may be needed (see Chapter 12, "When and How to Obtain a Release"). For example, you must obtain permission from the photographer and consent from the subject of the work if the photograph is to be used for commercial purposes, such as to convey a product endorsement.

If you have Internet access, visit the Stockphoto website, which has links to online directories of photographers (www.s2f.com/Stockphoto). Otherwise, contact the American Society of Media Photographers (ASMP) (609-799-8300) (www2.asmp.org/asmp), which has a searchable online membership directory, as well as a print version. If you are looking for a stock picture agency, the Picture Agency Council of America (PACA) publishes an excellent directory (PACA, Box 308, Northfield, MN 55057-0308) (800-457-7222). The Graphic Artists Guild (GAG) (212-463-7730) (www.gag.org) is an indispensable resource for locating particular illustrators, cartoonists, and, of course, graphic artists, many of whom also work as freelancers.

If you want to include charts or figures that appeared in a book or magazine, generally you'll need permission from the publisher, not the author. If you want to reprint an advertisement, you'll need permission from the advertiser, and, perhaps, the advertising agency. The first place to look is the *Standard Directory of Advertisers* and its companion volume, the *Standard Directory of Advertising Agencies* (National Register Publishing). Out of an abundance of caution, you should also check to determine whether the photographer or the illustrator retained any rights that may require additional clearances. Unfortunately, who controls rights to advertising photography is often unclear, because of the parties' confusion over copyright law and its ownership rules. You'll also need to clear the rights and obtain privacy releases if you intend to use a model's image for commercial purposes. Contact the Advertising Photographers of America (800-272-6264) for direct access to an advertising photographer.

TIP If you need help locating a particular image, or you want to delegate responsibility for photo research to someone else, consider using a professional picture researcher. In addition to lending you their sleuthing abilities and well-honed aesthetic sensibilities, photo researchers can help you establish a realistic photo permission budget. Contact the American Society of Picture Professionals (ASPP) (206-226-2121), which publishes a membership list, or consult *Literary Market Place*, which lists photo researchers.

6.4.4   Works of Fine Art

If you'd like to reproduce a copyrighted work of art, such as a painting, assume that you will need two sets of permissions. First, you will need to obtain rights from the person who owns the color transparency or digital representation of the painting you want to copy. Bear in mind that there may be several sources (e.g., museum, gallery, and/or collector) for a particular image. Second, provided the original painting is not in the public domain, you will need permission from the original artist or the artist's estate. Museums, galleries, and collectors, as a rule, do not automatically obtain copyright in the works they acquire. However, the museum, gallery, or collector who owns a particular work often controls access and, therefore, reproduction rights, even if the work is in the public domain. Remember, when you obtain permission to use a photograph or 35mm slide, you do not automatically obtain permission to reproduce the original visual image reproduced in that photograph or slide.

Permission requests should be directed to the museum, gallery, stock house, or collector controlling the access to the work, as well as to the artist if the work is in copyright. Make certain you ask the museum or other source whether this source controls the reproduction rights to the artist's work. If the source does not, contact the Visual Artists and Galleries Association (VAGA) (212-808-0616) or the Artists Rights Society (ARS) (212-420-9160). VAGA and ARS can help you locate an artist, or an artist's estate, anywhere in the world. VAGA and ARS are artists' rights organizations that grant licenses and distribute monies on behalf of their members. ARS tends to represent more Western European artists—such as Dali, Miro, and Picasso—than does VAGA.

 CAUTION It is your responsibility to determine whether additional permissions or releases are required. Some stock houses and museums, for example, will not tell you that you must obtain additional clearances yourself. Always ask whether additional permissions are required. If the respondent says no, get it in writing.

6.4.5   Music

If you want to reprint copyrighted song lyrics or music, you must contact the music publisher. Because different songs may share the same title, indicate both the title of the composition and the composer in your request. For the sake of clarity, provide the publisher with the exact measure numbers to be quoted, counting from the beginning of the work or movement. To locate the rights holder, contact either the American Society of Composers, Authors and Publishers (ASCAP) (212-621-6000) (www.ascap.com) or Broadcast Music, Inc. (BMI) (212-586-2000) (www.bmi.com). If you prefer, you may gain access to their song databases via the Internet. If you don't know which society a writer belongs to, look at the liner notes that accompanied the record, CD, or cassette.

6.4.6   Cartoon Characters and Licensed Characters

Literary characters, including animated cartoon characters, may be protected under both copyright and trademark law. Animated characters are generally licensed through film studios or television production companies. *The Hollywood Reporter Blu Book* (213-525-2000), a "Who's Who" in the entertainment industry, lists the names of studio personnel and business-affairs executives, as well as talent agents and their celebrity clients. *The Licensing Resource Directory* (203-256-4700) and *The EPM Licensing Letter Sourcebook* (212-941-0099) are also excellent resource guides. Both contain listings of licensees, licensors, and support organizations. If you are trying to locate a syndicated or editorial cartoonist, you might also try the Graphic Artists Guild (212-791-0330).

6.4.7   Stills from Motion Pictures and Television Programs

If a publicity still was distributed to the public without proper copyright notice prior to March 1, 1989 (the date the notice requirement was abolished), that publicity still is in the public domain for copyright purposes. To clear a still first published on or after March 1, 1989, however, depending on the usage, you may need to deal with both the subject of the photo and the photographer. However, where the subject of the photograph is a public figure, such as a politician or a well-known actor, provided the intended use is an editorial use, no release is required, although you will still need permission to reproduce the photograph from the copyright owner.

In the film and television industries, the production company generally owns the copyright in the picture or program. However, most national news programming is owned by the major TV networks, not production companies. Because the production company's name is usually given at the beginning of a film or at the end of a television program, identifying the owner is relatively easy. Those with Internet access can visit Screensite's website, which offers access to film and television resources throughout the World Wide Web (www.sa.ua.edu/screensite). Another useful website is the Internet Movie Database (us.imdb.com/search), which lists, among other things, the name of the production company associated with each film in its database.

6.4.8   Speeches

While truly extemporaneous speeches are not protected by copyright, prepared speeches are. To clear a speech, you need to locate the author of the
speech—who may not be the same person who delivered it. In addition, if
the speech was recorded simultaneously with its delivery, you must locate
and obtain permission from the owner of the sound or videotape recording,
provided you want to exploit the actual recording. Finally, if you plan to use
the audio or videotape recording of the speech for commercial purposes, you
will need a right-of-publicity release from the person who delivered the speech.
The right of publicity applies not only to people's likenesses, but also to their
voices and other identifiable characteristics. Start with the speech maker's
publicist, who may actually have written the speech. If the speech was recorded by a news organization, and you plan to use the actual speech, contact
that organization.

6.5   What Do I Do If I Still Can't Locate
the Rights Holder?

While locating a copyright owner may be as easy as finding the copyright
notice or credit line, sometimes you'll encounter difficulty, especially with
older works. If you need help, the U.S. Copyright Office may be able to tell
you whether the work was registered for copyright. If the work was registered
with the Copyright Office, you can also trace the chain of title by conducting
a copyright assignment search. Keep in mind that an assignment search will
not reveal unrecorded, or secret, assignments, or assignments that were recently
filed but not yet catalogued.

For an hourly fee, the Copyright Office (202-707-6850) will conduct a
search of its Catalog of Copyright Entries and will report back to you with
its findings, including the copyright owner's or assignee's address, and, in
some instances, the name of the authorized person or organization to contact
for permission to use the work. Copyright Office Circular R22, "How to
Investigate the Copyright Status of a Work," is reproduced in Appendix A.
You may also visit the Library of Congress's website or the Copyright Office
itself, at the James Madison Memorial Building, 101 Independence Avenue
SE, Washington, DC 20559-6000. The office is open to the public Monday
through Friday, 8:30 A.M. to 5 P.M., EST. Appendix B contains information
on Internet access to copyright information.

If you need further assistance in tracking down a copyright owner, there are professional copyright search firms, permission specialists, and copyright attorneys who can help. Search firms, such as Thomson & Thomson (800-356-8630) (www.thomson-thomsom.com), will determine whether a work has been registered for copyright. To the extent the information is available, these firms may also be able to tell you whether a copyright was renewed or the rights were transferred to another party. In addition, many search firms maintain private databases to help verify that the person purporting to license you the rights is the true owner. Additional listings of permission specialists can be found in *Literary Market Place* (LMP).

Be aware that copyright search reports do not draw conclusions about the copyright status of a work. The most crucial step is analyzing the information they have reported. Just as real estate lawyers review title documents, copyright attorneys review copyright reports and the underlying documents of title to determine whether the person claiming to have rights actually controls those rights. These attorneys can also tell you whether a title you are considering for your own work conflicts with a title for a prior work.

While a search of the Copyright Office records is very useful and in many cases will reveal the identity of the owner of a work, keep in mind that registration is *voluntary*. Therefore, many works may not be registered. Further, many works may be untitled or registered under a different title, making it impossible or at least difficult to locate in a copyright search. Therefore, while a copyright search is helpful, it is not always conclusive.

6.6 What If the Party That Grants Me Permission Isn't the Current Copyright Owner?

If you discover that the party who you believed had the right to grant you permission had actually transferred the copyright to someone else *before* granting you permission, you may still have a valid license, provided three conditions exist: (1) Permission was given on a nonexclusive basis (permission is usually granted nonexclusively); (2) permission was granted in writing and signed by the party granting it; and (3) at the time you received permission, the prior assignment was not recorded with the Copyright Office. Of course, if you had actual knowledge of the prior assignment at the time you received written permission, your permission would be invalid.

So what does this mean? It means you should get your permissions in writing. For example, if A transfers copyright ownership in her photos to B in January 1998, and then, in February 1998, A grants you written permission to use the photos in your book, and later, in March 1998, B records her assignment with the Copyright Office, you can continue to publish your book with the photos, because your permission grant was signed *before* B recorded her assignment from A. On the other hand, if A transfers copyright in her photos to B in January 1998, and B promptly records the assignment with the Copyright Office, and then in February 1998, A grants you written permission to use her photos on the cover of your book, you would *not* be allowed to continue to publish your book with the photos on the cover.

It is important to note that permission recipients do not have to record their assignments in order to prevail over a prior assignment. However, they must obtain written and signed permission grants to protect their rights.

6.7   What If I Can't Locate a Copyright Owner, but I Use the Material Anyway?

If you can't locate the owner of a copyright, and you use the material without permission, unless the use is a fair use, you will have infringed the owner's copyright. However, you can take some comfort in the fact that the Copyright Act treats good-faith infringers less harshly than bad-faith ones. Assuming that your infringement is discovered, provided you have taken diligent steps to locate the copyright owner, a court might only require that you pay a reasonable retroactive permission fee. However, nothing would prevent a copyright owner from suing you for injunctive relief, damages, attorneys' fees, and court costs for using the work without consent. Consequently, whenever you use a work, or a portion of a work, without permission, you risk legal liability, including the cost of defending a lawsuit.

6.8   Must Permission Be in Writing?

Permissions are contracts. While oral permissions are generally valid, it is a good idea to get your permissions in writing to avoid a later dispute over what rights were actually granted. In addition, in some states, oral permission may be revoked at any time before publication. Further, most publishers require authors to deliver copies of their permissions with their final manuscript. If you don't get your permissions in writing, you won't be able to satisfy your obligations to your publisher, and your work may go unpublished.

6.9 Once I Locate the Copyright Owner, How Do I Request Permission?

Once you've located the copyright owner, it is time to request permission. There are no right or wrong permission forms. However, many publishers have a standard packet that they provide to their authors that includes approved forms and permission guidelines. Because these forms (and guidelines) vary from publisher to publisher, ask your publisher for a copy of the most recent packet.

It is customary to mail the copyright owner a permission request letter, which the owner can sign and return to you to verify that permission has been granted. You should always include at least two and preferably three original permission request letters. This allows the rights holder, your publisher, and you to each retain an original. Additionally, you should always include a self-addressed, stamped envelope to facilitate the return of the signed permission request letter. For your convenience, we've included a sample permission request letter in Appendix C. This letter, which includes instructions, can be adapted to fit your particular needs.

Many publishers are now processing permission requests via e-mail. So, it may make sense to call first to see whether this is the preferred method of requesting permission.

6.9.1 Contents of a Permission Request Letter

Your permission request letter is a formal letter informing the copyright owner, or the owner's representative, that you would like to use the owner's material in your work. Once countersigned by the rights holder and returned to you, it is a binding contract. When sending a permission request letter, you must clearly and precisely identify the material for which you are seeking permission. For this reason, it might be helpful to attach to your request letter a photocopy of the article, quotation, diagram, illustration, or other material you propose to use. For your own record-keeping purposes, mark the corresponding manuscript page number at the top right-hand corner of your permission request letter.

The following information (to the extent it is applicable) about your work, the owner's work, and the scope of the rights you need should appear in your permission request letter.

Information about Your Work
- Your name and the title of your work
- The approximate number of pages and the tentative list price
- The tentative first printing and the projected publication, or on-sale, date
- The name of your publisher
- A description of your work (college textbook, hardcover, trade paperback, magazine article, etc.)
- Whether you intend to alter, edit, or otherwise change or adapt the material in question.

Information about the Owner's Work
- The author's, editor's, translator's, or artist's full name
- The title, edition, or volume number
- The copyright year
- The ISBN for books or the ISSN for magazines and journals
- The exact page numbers and clear identification of the materials desired, along with a photocopy of the material
- The figure or chart numbers, if relevant
- The size of the image in relation to your work (e.g., $1/4$ page, $1/2$ page)
- Whether the image will be reproduced in color or in black and white
- A copy of the copyright notice page or the title page of the original work containing the material you want to reprint

The Scope of the Rights You Need
- Media and formats
- Activities
- Territories
- Languages

Make certain that the permission you receive covers the full scope of your needs. The permission you receive should at least parallel what you promised your publisher. It should also be clear that you are allowed to assign the permission grant or license to others, such as your publisher. Thus, before asking for permission, review your publishing contract or talk to your editor to find out what rights you will need. Make certain your permission covers all territories, languages, media, markets, and editions covered by your publishing agreement. Anything less may not allow your publisher to exploit your work.

Be realistic when seeking permission. Blanket permission is seldom given, and a broadly worded permission can be costly. If you don't need particular rights, don't acquire them. However, keep in mind that rights not specifically granted cannot be used without further permission.

Usually, permission to use a copyrighted work is limited to one edition, or one-time use. Additional fees, based on a percentage of the original price, are required for each reuse or revision. Separate requests are usually required for electronic and Internet uses, too.

Following are two sample clauses requesting rights that you may adapt when requesting permission. The first request is very broad and will save you the effort of having to go back and clear additional rights at a later date. However, some rights holders may balk at signing it or charge you a very high fee. The second request is narrower in scope.

> I request the nonexclusive right to use the following material through-out the world, in all languages, in this and all subsequent editions and other derivative works published or prepared by [Pubco Publishers, Inc.] or its licensees, for the full term of copyright.

> I request the nonexclusive right to use the following material in the United States, its possessions and territories, and Canada, in the English language, in this and all subsequent editions of the work published or prepared by [Pubco Publishers, Inc.] or its licensees for the full term of copyright.

TIP Make sure you obtain a grant of rights broad enough to encompass all contemplated uses of your work. For example, if you plan to publish your work in foreign-language editions, make sure your permission forms give you the right to use the preexisting material in foreign-language editions.

6.9.2 The Permission Log

It is helpful to maintain a permission log when creating your work. (See Appendix C, Form I, for a sample log.) The log should describe the sources (including author, title, and copyright holder) and materials incorporated in your work, as well as actual people and entities described in your work. The log will become a checklist for you when your work is completed, so that you will be able to keep track of which necessary permissions and releases you have and have not yet obtained.

Your log should contain the following information:

1. The title of the source material or preexisting work and the corresponding manuscript page number
2. The source of the material (including the name of the author, illustrator, or photographer from whom a license or permission may be required)
3. The name and address of the publisher of the preexisting work
4. The date on which permission was requested
5. The date when permission was granted
6. The scope of rights granted
7. The permission fee that was due and when it was paid
8. The number of complimentary copies of your work that are due on publication
9. The required credits and acknowledgments for materials

A separate log should be kept for all recognizable people, places, or things depicted in your work, for purposes of vetting (evaluating) your manuscript for possible libel or right-of-privacy issues (see Chapter 10, "How to Minimize Libel Claims").

6.9.3   Credit

Credit, or a brief statement of where borrowed material came from, is usually specified by contract, with the precise credit wording stipulated by the copyright holder of the borrowed material. Thus, make sure all contributions are properly credited by double-checking all permission forms to make sure you comply with credit obligations. A convenient form for tracking credit lines stipulated by copyright owners is located in Appendix C. In the case of an image, a credit next to the image may be required. Otherwise, an acknowledgment section at the front or back of your book will usually suffice. For example:

> The authors are grateful to the following authors, publishers, copyright holders, and others for granting permission to use excerpts from the following works:
>
> Righter, I. M., *The Word Book*, © 1998 by I. M. Righter. Reprinted by permission of Prose Press, a division of the Pubco Publishing Group, Inc.

Make sure that proper copyright notices (©, year of first publication, and name of copyright owner) appear next to all supplemental material such as charts, photographs, or the complete text of passages such as song lyrics.

Sample Photo Credits

1. Photo by _____, courtesy of _____.

2. Courtesy of _____.

Sample Text Credit

Reprinted by permission of _____.

6.9.4   Payment Obligations

Honor your payment obligations, including any promise to provide complimentary copies of the finished work. If you do not pay the agreed-upon fee, or you otherwise fail to live up to your obligations, including credit obligations, the person granting you permission may have the right to terminate or revoke the permission (or release) and to sue you for copyright infringement, defamation, or even invasion of privacy. See Appendix C, Form K, for a sample complimentary copy form to help you keep track of this obligation.

6.9.5   Miscellaneous

Check your permission agreements to make certain you have received the rights you requested. If the permission agreement does not expressly state that you have been granted a particular right, you probably do not have it. If the rights holder fails to respond, send a follow-up letter, attaching your original correspondence for ease of reference. As rule, the larger the publisher (or other rights holder), the longer is the wait. In fact, a four- to six-week wait is not unusual. If you are dealing with older material, the publisher will probably have to review the status of the copyright to see whether it has authority to grant permission; such a review will take even longer to complete. Granting permission is not a mechanical process.

You must get an affirmative response to your permission request letter. Silence does not constitute permission. Be prepared to follow up on all permission requests with a telephone call. See Appendix C, Form I, for sample permission summary form.

6.9.6   Delivery of Forms

You should deliver all permissions to your publisher when you deliver your manuscript. Check with your publisher for the preferred delivery procedure for permissions. Some publishers require authors to deliver their permissions to a special permissions editor, separately from the manuscript. You should also check with your publisher to determine whether the permission must be provided in any particular order or sequence. For example, some publishers require authors to identify each permission according to the page on which the material appears.

6.10   Negotiation Tips

Obtaining permission is an art, not a science, so be prepared to negotiate. Because usage fees vary with considerations such as the amount taken, the language, the territory, the intended use, and the period of use (and even the user), if you don't need certain rights, don't try to acquire them. However, when employing this tactic, make sure your publisher (or agent) approves. If you want to extend the scope of the permission license at a later date, you can agree on a set price (usually based on a percentage of the original fee) up front.

Be aware that not-for-profit organizations often receive more favorable terms than do commercial entities. If you or your publisher is a nonprofit organization, make it known. Permission may be granted for free.

Many freelance authors and artists handle their own permissions. When negotiating with them, make an effort to understand their real concerns. You may be surprised to learn that they are more concerned about credit, artistic integrity, or approval of the context in which their work is used than they are about the permission fee. Similarly, if freelancers balk at signing a work for hire agreement, don't jump to any conclusions. Again, their real concern may be credit, or the right to include the work in their professional portfolio. These concerns can be addressed with a little simple contract drafting (see Chapter 7, "Dealing with Collaborators and Contributors").

If you reach a deadlock on price, politely remind the content provider that he or she is not the only fish in the sea (that is, assuming there is an equally qualified content provider waiting in the wings). You may have more bargaining power than you give yourself credit for. Another tactic is to ask the question, "How did you arrive at that price?" Knowledge is power, and price breakdowns allow you to challenge assumptions. Most importantly, be courteous and have patience.

If you are uncomfortable with negotiating, there are professionals who will do the dirty work for you. Permission specialists, who have established relationships with many content providers, will obtain permission from copyright owners and other proprietors on your behalf. They can also help you establish a reasonable permission budget. Depending on the nature of the project, they will work on either a flat-fee or an hourly basis. You will find permission specialists listed in *Literary Market Place* under "Services and Suppliers" (see Appendix E).

6.10.1 Cost-Saving Strategies

Of course, another way to keep fees down is to use public domain materials. For example, if you want to reprint a passage from the medieval epic *The Song of Roland* or some other classic, you have two choices—use a public domain translation, or a recently copyrighted one. (As we pointed out in Chapter 2, translations are copyrightable derivative works.) If you insist on using the copyrighted version, you might try to negotiate a break in the permission fee by making the publisher aware that you are prepared to use the public domain version if you can't arrive at a reasonable permission fee. Smaller publishers tend to respond better to this kind of argument than do larger ones (see Chapter 4, "What's in the Public Domain?").

If you are purchasing a large number of images, purchase them from one or two stock agencies, and ask for a quantity discount. Because pricing in the stock-image industry is unpredictable, shop around. Fees for similar images can vary widely.

Another cost-saving measure is to use royalty-free clip art, which can be purchased in book form, on diskette, or on CD-ROM. Be certain to read the small print on the shrink-wrap license or insert that accompanies any copyright-free or royalty-free material. There may be contractual limitations on permissible use beyond a certain point. Moreover, if there are any recognizable people, places, or things, you may still need to obtain a right-of-privacy, right-of-publicity, or other form of release, even though the content is copyright free (see Chapter 11, "Basics of Publicity and Privacy").

Finally, some grantors offer a discount on fees paid within a certain number of days, but they don't always advertise this fact. For example, as this is being written, the McGraw-Hill Companies require payment of permission fees within 60 days but offer a 10 percent discount on fees paid within 45 days.

6.10.2   Permission Fees

The broader the rights, the higher the fee. Because fees charged depend on the material used, the manner of use, and even the user, it is hard to make generalizations about permission fees.

Factors that may influence permission fees include:

- The print run or circulation
- The size of the excerpt
- The size of the image in relation to the page
- The intended use of the image (e.g., interior use, cover use, black-and-white vs. color reproduction, editorial vs. advertising vs. corporate use
- The importance of the licensed work to your project
- The method of exploitation (e.g., media, platforms, activities, channels of trade)
- The nature of the user (e.g., profit vs. nonprofit, scholarly use)
- The intended territory of use
- The languages sought
- The importance of the work or of the author and the goodwill that the licensor will receive, given the association with your project
- When the original work was published
- Whether the original work was a best-seller

Permission fees are usually one-time lump-sum payments, with additional compensation for subsequent new uses not originally contemplated by the parties. Royalties, which are fees based on usage or sales, are the exception, not the rule, for nonexclusive permission grants. Due to the ease with which copyrighted material can be digitally reproduced, many grantors are not currently granting rights for online use.

Following are examples of representative permission fees and industry practices as of the writing of this book, as the fees relate to text, illustrations (e.g., photos), and fine art.

6.10.2.1   Text

By way of illustration, the Dow Jones Company (800-843-0008)—publishers of *The Wall Street Journal* (WSJ) and *Barrons*—publishes a rate card. Prices quoted are for printings of books over 3,000 copies as of January 1997.

1. Front-page article from any section written by a WSJ reporter, using six paragraphs or more: $240

2. Any inside article using six paragraphs or more: $180
3. Using one to six paragraphs from any article: $87
4. Using a table or graph: $110

For printings between 1,000 and 3,000 copies, Dow Jones charges a flat fee of $90 per article, table, or graph. For printings of less than 1,000 copies, the fee drops to $60 per item.

Some publications, such as *Time* and *Newsweek*, specifically prohibit adapting or paraphrasing, although this may not be supported by the fair use doctrine. *Advertising Age*, and many book publishers, do not charge if you use very small amounts of material, provided that permission is requested. If you look on the copyright page of some books, you may find a permission notice stating that you can use up to 500 words in the context of a critical review or essay about the book. This, in essence, is the publisher's acknowledgment that fair use applies in such situations.

An excellent guide to pricing is *The NWU Guide to Freelance Rates and Standard Practices*, prepared by the National Writers Union (NWU) (distributed by Writer's Digest Books). *Kohn on Music Licensing*, published by Aspen Law & Business, is another useful book that lists typical license fees charged by music publishers for song lyrics. According to *Kohn*, the range for reprinting song lyrics runs between $25 and $250, plus two copies of the book. Similarly, the right to reprint a poem in an anthology will cost you between $50 and $300, plus two or three complimentary copies of the book. As these examples show, the party granting permission will often want to receive complimentary copies of your work when it is finally published.

6.10.2.2 *Dealing with Stock Picture Agencies and Other Photographic Collections*

Stock houses, which acquire the right to sell photographs and other images from many different sources, usually charge one fee for reproduction rights and another fee for the rental of transparencies or the production of materials. Generally, prints, transparencies, and diskettes must be returned within a set time period, or penalties are incurred. Also, you should expect to pay a nonrefundable photo-research fee. Often, this fee can be applied against your ultimate purchase.

Pricing among stock houses varies greatly, depending on usage, ranging on average from $75 to $600 (more if used for a picture book) for an interior image for a book. Factors influencing price include the size of the reproduction ($^1\!/_4$ page, $^1\!/_2$ page, etc.); the press run; the type of book; the use of color versus black and white; and the rights sought (e.g., North American vs. world rights). Bear in mind that an image used on a jacket or cover commands a higher price than does an interior image.

Using "North American rights" or "one country, one language rights" as a benchmark, expect to pay an additional 100 percent to 150 percent of the original benchmark price for "one-time world rights, one language," and up to 200 percent for "world rights, all languages." Don't confuse "world rights" with "world rights, *all languages*." There are many ways to skin the copyright cat. Make sure you specify both the geographic area of distribution and the languages. Precision counts! If you purchase rights à la carte, for each new or foreign-language edition, expect to pay 25 percent to 50 percent above the benchmark price. If you know what you need, and you can afford it, purchase it up front. It's usually cheaper that way. Volume discounts may also be available. Therefore, it is a good idea, if feasible, to purchase all of your images from one or two sources.

Many people are shocked to learn that the stock agency rental agreement they've signed does not necessarily give them the unfettered right to reproduce the transparency they have purchased. What stock houses, and some museums, forget to tell you is that your payment covers only the lending of prints or transparencies. You may need a second set of permissions, or releases, to use the material, or subject matter, depicted in the photograph. Thus, it is your responsibility to determine whether publication will infringe any copyright holders' rights. Helpful books include *Stock Photography: The Complete Guide* (Writer's Digest Books), *Pricing Photography* (Allworth Press), and *Negotiating Stock Photo Prices*, all of which include average price lists. *Negotiating Stock Photo Prices*, which is an excellent guide, is available direct from the publisher by mail. Call 301-251-0720 to order a copy. An indispensable book is *The Graphic Artists Guild Handbook: Pricing and Ethical Guidelines* (North Lights Books), which lists comparative fees for illustrations, graphic design, cartooning, and so on. For information about the stock picture industry, contact the Picture Agency Council of America (PACA) (800-457-PACA) (www.pacaoffice.org), which also publishes a directory.

TIP ☞ Many image libraries have moved online, which means you can now search for a particular image with a few clicks of your mouse. High-quality digital images can be downloaded as files or sent to you via floppy disk, or simply obtained in transparency form. For example, the Bettmann Archive (212-777-6200) (www.corbis.com) and Archive Photos (212-620-3955) (www.history.com), both known for their high-quality historical images, have searchable websites. Many stock photo agencies also produce CD-ROM catalog disks, which contain low-resolution composition-quality images for reference purposes.

6.10.2.3 Fine Art

As is the case for stock photography, the pricing of fine art depends on usage. For the right to use a fine-art reproduction of a well-known European abstract artist in the interior of a book with an initial print run of 5,000 copies, expect to pay approximately $100 to $150 for one-time U.S. rights. If the book goes back to press, or the image is reused in a foreign edition, you will be required to pay an additional fee. Similarly, English-language rights outside the United States may cost an additional 150 percent of the original price. With respect to world rights, in all languages, add up to 200 percent of what you originally paid for U.S. rights. As you can see, fees are negotiable—set on a case-by-case basis, depending on the rights sought and the configuration of the particular project.

It is worth noting that most publishers encourage their authors to acquire broad permission rights. While this gives publishers the flexibility to market your work, it also runs up the cost of permissions, which the author, not the publisher, must pay for. Discuss with your editor what exclusions, if any, can be made in your permission request letter.

 CAUTION Even if you've paid a permission fee, unless you've negotiated for reuse rights, you've only received one-time, nonexclusive rights in a specific medium for a limited time, in a particular territory, in a specific language. If you exceed the scope of your license, you are an infringer.

In addition to obtaining copyright permissions, it is also important to obtain appropriate releases and consents from people interviewed or depicted in your work. Interview releases, which are not legally required, protect you against media perils such as liability for invasion of the right of privacy, for libel, and for breach of contract (see Chapter 9, "Basics of Libel Law," and Chapter 11, "Basics of Publicity and Privacy").

CHECKLIST: **Getting Permission**

- ☐ Is the work, or its constituent parts, protected by copyright? As a general rule, anything published or registered more than 75 years ago is in the public domain. (The publication date of a work published in the United States can often be determined by looking at the date in the copyright notice.)
- ☐ Are you using the author's expression, or solely the underlying facts?
- ☐ Is the nature and amount of copying consistent with fair use?
- ☐ Is the work, or its component parts, protected by some other theory of intellectual property, such as trademark and unfair competition law, or the dual rights of publicity and privacy?
- ☐ Have you made any promises to anyone, either orally or in writing, not to reprint or reveal certain information?
- ☐ Is the material unpublished, or subject to contractual restrictions?
- ☐ Has material from another publisher, or other source, been incorporated in the material you are excerpting? If so, you may need permission from that source, too.
- ☐ Have you allowed enough time, and set aside a sufficient budget, to secure all necessary permissions? Delays are inevitable, and permission fees are likely to exceed your initial expectation.
- ☐ Have you properly identified the rights owner for the material you wish to use?
- ☐ Does more than one party control the rights? Remember that copyrights can be owned by multiple parties, requiring multiple permissions to use a single work.
- ☐ Has your publisher reviewed your permission and release forms?
- ☐ Does your permission request seek rights to the same territories, markets, and editions you granted to your publisher?
- ☐ Does your permission grant address the following rights issues?
  - • Media and formats
  - • Geographic territories
  - • Languages
  - • Reprints, revisions, and revised editions
  - • Credit obligations and notices
- ☐ Can you assign the permission license or release form you've received?
- ☐ Are VIPs, celebrities, cartoon characters, or licensed characters visually depicted? If so, do you need a release?
- ☐ Did you get an affirmative response to your permission request? Silence does not constitute permission.

☐ Did you quote yourself? If a different publisher controls the rights to your original work, unless the use is a fair use, you need permission.

☐ Do you have a signed work for hire agreement (signed *before* the creation of the work) for all work that was specially created at your request?

7

Dealing with Collaborators and Contributors

You should be greatly concerned about who owns the work you specially commission (or who owns the rights for projects on which you work with others). For example, unless there is a special kind of agreement in place before any work begins, someone who contributes material to your new book can, in theory, sell that same material elsewhere without your permission. Worse still, if there is no written agreement, and you want to adapt that material or publish it elsewhere, you may need that person's permission. Similarly, if you hire someone to illustrate one of your short stories, unless there is a written agreement that says otherwise, you may be surprised to learn that the illustrator has become your coauthor. These seemingly odd results follow from the fact that under copyright law, authors, artists, and musicians are presumed to own the copyright in the works they create. The best way to avoid these problems is by having a *written* agreement in place before any work begins.

7.1 *Do I Own the Work I've Paid For?*

You do not necessarily own the specially commissioned work you've paid for. If a work doesn't qualify as a work for hire, you may not own the work or even have the exclusive right to use it. However, you may have an implied license to use it, but without a written agreement, the scope of those rights is unclear. One way to avoid this situation is to use an appropriate work for hire agreement, discussed in more detail in Section 7.2.

7.2 *What Is a Work for Hire?*

One way to acquire rights is by license. With a license, you do not obtain total ownership of the final work, but rather certain limited rights to use it. These limited rights can be either exclusive or nonexclusive. As a rule, however, hiring parties prefer to obtain rights on a work for hire basis (shorthand for work made for hire). With a work for hire, the hiring party steps into the shoes of the creator and becomes the author of the work, for copyright purposes. With a work for hire. all of the attributes of copyright ownership—including credit and control—vest in the hiring party.

There are only two situations in which a work for hire can exist:

1. A work prepared by an employee within the scope his or her employment

2. A work created by an independent contractor upon special request, *provided* certain conditions are satisfied

Under the 1976 Copyright Act, for a work created by an independent contractor (or freelancer) to qualify as a work for hire, three specific conditions must be satisfied:

1. The work must be specially ordered or commissioned. In other words, the independent contractor is paid to create something new (as opposed to being paid for a preexisting work).

2. Prior to commencement of work, the parties must acknowledge, in writing, *signed* by *both* of them, that the work will be considered a work for hire.

3. The work must fall within at least one of the following nine narrow statutory categories of commissioned works listed in the Copyright Act: (1) a translation, (2) a contribution to a motion picture or other audiovisual work, (3) a contribution to a collective work (such as a magazine), (4) an atlas, (5) a compilation, (6) an instructional text, (7) a test, (8) some answer material for a test, (9) or a supplementary work. (The Copyright Act defines a *supplementary work* as "a work prepared for publication as a secondary adjunct to a work by another author for the purpose of introducing, concluding, illustrating, explaining, revising, commenting upon, or assisting in the use of the other works." Common examples of supplementary works include forewords, afterwords, pictorial illustrations, maps, charts, tables, editorial notes, bibliographies, appendixes, and indexes.)

As this is being written, the law is unsettled over the issue of whether a work for hire agreement signed *after* work has begun is valid. However, the authors strongly recommend that all work for hire agreements be signed *before* any work commences. Without an agreement signed by both parties before work begins, the status of the parties' relationship (and the copyright) may be in dispute.

Because a work does not become a work for hire unless the work falls within one of these nine narrow categories, a written work for hire agreement does not always result in a work becoming a work for hire. For example, a novel can never be a work for hire, because it's not on the short list of nine works eligible for work for hire status by nonemployees.

Bear in mind that what constitutes a work made for hire under the 1909 Copyright Act (which governs works created before January 1, 1978) differs significantly from what constitutes a work made for hire under the 1976 Copyright Act. Under the old Copyright Act, the key inquiry was whether the employer had the right to direct and supervise the manner in which the author performed her or his work.

7.3   Why Is It Important to Have a Backup Copyright Assignment?

Because merely stating that a work is a work for hire may not be enough (e.g., it may not fall within one of the nine categories, or qualify as a specially commissioned work), a well-drafted work for hire agreement should also contain a backup copyright assignment (see Appendix C, Form G, "Simple 'Work Made for Hire' Agreement" and Form H, "Short-Form Copyright Assignment"). With an assignment, the original creator remains the author, but you own all the rights.

7.4   Are Work for Hire Agreements Fair?

While asking a freelance writer, or other creator, to work on a work for hire basis is inappropriate in certain situations (e.g., freelance magazine articles), in other situations, it is equally unreasonable for a freelance contributor to seek compensation on the basis of a work's earnings. For example, advertising copywriters, corporate public-relations writers, indexers, researchers (to the extent their work is copyrightable), and ghostwriters should be willing to part with their copyright interests for a lump-sum payment, provided there's adequate compensation.

7.5   What Are the Dangers of Work for Hire from a Hiring Party's Perspective?

Characterizing a work as a work for hire could impose on an employer certain obligations relating to state workers' compensation coverage, unemployment compensation, and other benefits for workers, as well as state and federal tax consequences. Therefore, consult with your tax advisor before commissioning a work for hire—both copyright and employee-benefit issues may be involved.

Take special care when working with independent contractors or freelancers. Because independent contractors may hire other independent contractors (subcontractors), it is imperative that you secure rights to those materials, too. For example, if you work with a graphic artist to create a dust jacket, the final work may contain illustrations or photographs that belong to a third party. Similarly, if someone prepares an introduction to your book and quotes extensively from someone else's copyrighted work, the author of that "embedded" work may have a claim against you if you don't obtain proper permission. Therefore, when working with contributors, make sure the responsibility for clearing rights to any work embedded in their work is clearly spelled out. Also, bear in mind that any permissions obtained by an independent contractor working on your behalf must specifically state that those rights are transferable.

One way to make contributors mindful of what you need is by asking them to *represent* in writing that their work is original and not in the public domain. Also, have them *warrant* that their work does not infringe any copyright or other proprietary rights. To further limit your risk, ask them to indemnify and reimburse you for any damages or costs you incur as a result of any breach of their representations and warranties.

7.6   Works Created by Employees

A work created by an employee within the scope of his or her employment is automatically considered a work for hire and is owned by the employer. No written agreement is needed. Unlike works created by independent contractors, these works do not have to fall into one of the nine special statutory categories to be considered works for hire. Of course, not everything created by an employee belongs to his or her employer. If a poem is written at home, it is not a work for hire, because it wasn't created within the scope of employment.

7.6.1   Independent Contractor or Employee?

Sometimes disputes arise over whether a work was created by an independent contractor or an employee. As a practical matter, nonemployees are presumed to own their copyrights, absent an agreement to the contrary. Therefore, how a person is classified determines copyright ownership.

The term *employee* is a legal term of art without precise definition. What you call that person, or how you classify that relationship, is not determinative. However, a worker is most likely to be classified as an employee if the person who pays the worker has the legal right to control the "method and result" of the individual's work and provides worker benefits. Among the factors courts examine to determine whether someone is an employee are these:

- The skill required
- Whether payment is made on a daily, weekly, or monthly basis
- Whether the worker works on the hiring party's premises
- Whether the hiring party has the right to assign additional projects to the worker
- The duration of the relationship between the parties
- Who determines when and how long the worker must work
- Who provides the worker's tools, materials, and other equipment
- Whether the worker generally works for one business at a time
- Who hires and pays assistants
- Whether employee benefits are paid by the hiring party
- The tax treatment of the worker

TIP Unlike specially commissioned works, for works where a traditional employer-employee relationship exists, no work for hire agreement is needed. However, to avoid any ambiguity, it's a good idea to include a statement in the employment agreement acknowledging that any work created in the scope of employment will be considered a work for hire.

An important issue that arises in the context of employer-employee relationships is the ownership of works prepared after hours, or outside the scope of employment. Under the Copyright Act, work products prepared outside the scope of the worker's job are not generally considered works for hire. Therefore, employers may have to negotiate for such materials separately.

7.6.2   What about Works by Two or More Authors?

Whenever two parties work together without an agreement, they run the risk of being considered joint authors if their contributions are independently copyrightable. While half a copyright is better than none, under copyright law, a relatively small contribution may entitle a contributor to an equal share of profits. Because no written agreement is needed to create a joint work, you must be extremely careful when working with collaborators. Absent a written agreement, ownership is governed by copyright law and the courts, and the result may not be to your liking.

7.6.3   What Is Joint Work?

The formal legal definition of a *joint work* is a "work prepared by two or more authors with the intention that their contributions be merged into inseparable or interdependent parts of a unitary whole." The authors do not have to work together at the same time. The key to a joint work is the authors' intention at the time the work is created. If there is no written agreement, courts sometimes look for evidence of billing or credit to determine intent.

In order to qualify as a joint work, each author's contribution must also be independently copyrightable. In general, ideas, suggestions, and refinements standing alone are not protected under the Copyright Act. Therefore, a copyeditor's or proofreader's comments or suggestions do not entitle them to half a copyright.

If the *intent* to create a joint work is missing, it is possible that a court might find that the work qualifies as a work for hire, or perhaps a collective or derivative work, discussed in Chapter 2.

7.6.4   How Do You Avoid Accidental Coauthorship?

To avoid any misunderstanding, whenever you work with editors, artists, illustrators, researchers, indexers, or other contributors, it is important to have a short, written release that expressly states that their work shall be considered a work for hire for copyright purposes. This should be signed before work begins. This ensures that you, as the hiring party, own and control the finished work. As a fallback position, in the event the work is determined not to be a work for hire, it is important that you obtain a written assignment of all the rights. Similarly, it is prudent for true collaborators to have a collaboration agreement—preferably drafted by an attorney—defining the parties' respective rights and obligations.

TIP
☞

Because even a relatively small creative contribution may entitle a would-be collaborator to an equal interest in your work, it is important to have a written contract defining each party's rights and obligations whenever you work with others.

7.6.5 Among Coauthors, Who Has the Right to Grant Permissions?

Unless there is an agreement to the contrary, under the laws of joint authorship, each coauthor may (without consent of the other) grant permission to use the joint work on a *nonexclusive* basis. Problems may arise if worldwide rights are needed, because the laws of some countries require that all coauthors consent to a license. Similarly, under U.S. law, all coauthors must consent to an *exclusive* license. Where possible, obtain permission from all the co-owners, especially if you are clearing either worldwide rights or rights outside the United States.

7.6.6 When Is the Best Time to Prepare a Collaboration Agreement?

The best time to address the major issues confronting collaborators is before the actual collaboration process takes place. Although coauthors might not feel comfortable discussing long-term financial issues or the eventuality of a dispute or even the death of a partner, it is always easier (and less expensive) to deal with these issues up front, before the collaboration begins, rather than later, after a dispute arises.

CHECKLIST: Works Made for Hire and Joint Works

☐ Unless authors or artists sign away their rights, or qualify as employees, they own and control the copyrights to their work.

☐ A work created within the normal scope of an author's or artist's regular employment is automatically owned by the employer and does not require a written agreement.

☐ Workers are either employees or independent contractors. Determining which label applies is not always easy. The closer the relationship comes to regular, salaried employment, the more likely the work product would be considered a work for hire.

- [ ] Usually, three attributes must exist before a work created by a nonemployee will be classified as a work for hire: (1) both parties must sign an agreement *before* any work starts; (2) the agreement must state that the work will be regarded as work for hire; and (3) the work must fall within one of nine narrow categories listed in the Copyright Act.
- [ ] The nine special categories of work for hire are
  - A contribution to a collective work (e.g., newspapers, magazines, other periodicals, anthologies, encyclopedias)
  - A contribution to a motion picture or other audiovisual work
  - A translation
  - A compilation (e.g., catalogs, databases, directories, guidebooks, maps, price lists)
  - A test
  - Answer material for a test
  - An instructional text
  - An atlas
  - Supplementary work (e.g., forewords, afterwords, pictorial illustrations, maps, charts, tables, editorial notes, bibliographies, appendixes, indexes)
- [ ] Even if a work falls within one of the nine categories, you may not have a work for hire unless the work for hire agreement is signed *before* any work begins. Most courts say that once work begins, it is too late to create a work for hire.
- [ ] When drafting a work for hire agreement, seek a simultaneous assignment of copyright. This will come in handy later if, for any reason, the work is found not to be a work for hire.
- [ ] Don't rely on freelancers to voluntarily obtain written permissions and release forms from third parties; make such forms a delivery requirement.
- [ ] Whenever two parties work together without an agreement, joint authorship may be inferred from the circumstances. Therefore, before any work is begun, a well-drafted work for hire agreement should be signed by the parties.

8

Multimedia Clearances

Creating a multimedia or mixed-media work (whether an educational CD-ROM, an entertainment DVD, or a website combining text, graphics, audio and/or video) presents unique and challenging permission issues. More so than with print permissions, when dealing with multimedia permissions, you will often find yourself interacting with several parties just to clear a single work. This chapter provides an overview of some of the complicated issues involved in multimedia clearances. It is intended both to help you get started and to alert you to the kinds of issues and challenges ahead. Because of the complexity of the issues involved, you should consider seeking the expertise of a rights-clearance expert or an attorney experienced in multimedia law.

CAUTION If you are acquiring the rights to use preexisting material, you may want to make certain that the party licensing the rights originally received rights broad enough to encompass multimedia. Protracted legal battles have been fought over whether old contracts contemplated uses for works beyond what was envisioned by the parties when the agreements were first signed.

With this in mind, when licensing rights, ask the granting party to warrant that it controls the rights being licensed. If possible, you should also get the licensing party to indemnify you (compensate you for damages and attorneys' fees) if they breach their warranties. Just as in buying a house, you want to make sure you are getting clear title to the material around which you are building your multimedia project.

8.1 Key Terms Covered by a Multimedia Permission

The following are some fundamental issues that every multimedia permission license should address.

8.1.1 Platforms and Markets

Because multimedia technology is constantly changing, rights holders are sometimes reluctant to grant broad rights. If broad rights are granted, they often command a substantial fee. Rights may be restricted in any number of ways. For example, cross-platform permissions are not typically granted. *Platform* refers to the medium (e.g., IBM compatible versus Apple computers), not the message. Sometimes a rights holder may be willing to grant rights only for certain hardware devices or software formats. As a rule, titles are prepared for specific platforms that are incompatible with one another. Some licenses may contain a right of first negotiation for unsecured platforms, or an option whereby the multimedia producer obtains the right to obtain further platform rights for a specific period of time. Licenses can also be granted on an exclusive or a nonexclusive basis, or they can be restricted to a particular market or mode of distribution (e.g., nonretail markets only).

8.1.2 Portion Limitations

Keep in mind that most rights holders prefer to limit the length, or portion, of the material you can use. This is because they do not want the new use to supplant the market for the original work. This is especially true for music and video clips. When licensing music, be prepared to describe how the music will be used.

If you plan to alter or modify a preexisting work, unless the work is in the public domain, or the use is a fair use, make certain to obtain express permission to do so.

8.1.3 Territory and Language

Territorial and language restrictions, as well as term limits, will also apply in most cases. Be aware of what those restrictions are, and make sure they do not hamper your ability to market your finished product. On the other hand, don't be overambitious and try to clear all rights in all territories, or all languages up front. The costs for such clearance will be astronomical.

8.1.4   Approvals

Rights holders may request approvals, which will inevitably slow up your production process. Resist giving such approval rights if possible. You do not want to be in a position where the entire work is completed but cannot be distributed because the rights holders don't like the finished product for purely subjective reasons. Instead of offering final approval rights, provide a detailed description or outline of the work, and agree to adhere to it.

Besides getting permission from the copyright owner, you may also need to obtain the consent of other individuals to use the licensed content. For example, if recognizable individuals, or trademarks, are depicted or incorporated in the licensed material, depending on the context, releases may be also needed (see Chapter 11, "Basics of Publicity and Privacy").

8.1.5   Credit

A key term of most negotiations is credit. Precise wording, including size, prominence, placement, and even duration, must be specified and complied with.

8.1.6   Fees

Like everything in life, the terms and conditions you are offered are subject to negotiation. While some terms may not be negotiable, many content providers are willing to compromise on certain issues, including price.

The key to pricing is the nature of the licensed work (backlist title or frontlist best-seller?) and the scope of the rights needed. Therefore, in order for rights holders to quote you a price, you must disclose to them how you plan to use their work. Among the factors influencing multimedia fees are the duration of the license, the geographic scope of the use, the nature of the use (e.g., background use, advertising use), and the platforms or devices licensed.

While it is not uncommon in print publishing to pay on publication, most copyright owners won't agree to this clause in multimedia agreements. However, if you use less than you planned, don't be shy about asking for a rebate. After all, if the usage increased, the grantor wouldn't be embarrassed to raise the fee.

When negotiating for multimedia rights, remember that multimedia works are nonlinear, containing pathways that the user may never explore. If the work you are licensing will be seldom seen or accessed, the fee you pay should reflect that.

One way to tame costs is to use royalty-free content from stock picture agencies (stock houses) and production music libraries. Flexibility is also very important. If you must have a particular image, clip, or song, you place yourself at a disadvantage. Due to the high cost of locating material, it is often advisable to limit yourself to one or two sources of material. By working with just one or two stock picture houses, you may be eligible to receive volume discounts.

8.2   Obtaining the Proper Rights

Unless you create your own content (e.g., text, photos, illustrations, animation, music), the first step in producing a multimedia work is identifying and locating the holders of the rights you need. Because any one work may contain layers and layers of rights, special attention must be paid to analyzing each element that makes up that work. Obtaining rights to one element does not automatically give you rights to use another. Rights must be assembled and cleared piecemeal. For example, if you plan to use a film clip that contains music, you need permission from the copyright holder of the film, from everyone seen or heard in the clip, from the musicians, and from the composer of the underlying music, as well as from various unions and guilds.

Here are some important issues to consider when licensing specific types of content, including music and audio clips, film and TV clips, photos and other artwork, cartoon characters, and text.

8.2.1   Music and Audio Clips

Multiple sets of rights must be cleared to use a piece of preexisting music because recorded music is subject to at least two copyrights: copyright in the underlying words and music, and copyright in the sound recording. In addition, performers have a right to control the commercial exploitation of their actual performances. Most writers and composers assign their copyrights to music publishers. Sound-recording copyrights are generally owned by record companies or producers.

Tip	If you use music or lyrics without permission, don't rely on the fair use defense. When it comes to music, fair use is construed narrowly. Courts have held that using just three words and accompanying music may, under certain circumstances, constitute copyright infringement.

Following are discussions of the types of music and sound-recording clearances and related issues you may need to consider for a multimedia work.

8.2.1.1 Synchronization and Videogram Licenses

A *synchronization ("synch") license* allows you to use music in combination with TV, motion-picture, or moving images. Synch rights, which are not mentioned in the Copyright Act, must be obtained from the owner of the copyright in the underlying musical composition (i.e., the composer and lyricist) before you use the music and corresponding images in your multimedia production. *Videogram licenses* are used in connection with home video devices, such as videocassettes and videodiscs. Synch and videogram licenses can be obtained from the copyright owner or through the Harry Fox Agency, Inc. (212-370-5330).

8.2.1.2 Mechanical Licenses

A *mechanical license* permits you to mechanically reproduce and distribute phonorecords (which includes audio CDs and cassettes). However, as a general rule, if a song is used in synchronization with a visual or moving image, *no* mechanical license is required. Only a synch license is needed in that case. The only exception to this rule involves multimedia titles that can be used in audio-only or multimedia modes, in which case you will need a mechanical license too. If you need a mechanical license, contact the Harry Fox Agency, Inc. (212-370-5330), which acts as a central clearinghouse for both synch and mechanical licenses.

8.2.1.3 Master-Use Licenses

If you want to use a particular performance by a recording artist, you may need a master-use license. *Master-use licenses* are issued by the artist's record company, the address of which is usually printed on the insert found in the CD jewel or cassette box.

8.2.1.4 Union Fees

After you've obtained your licenses, you still have additional considerations. Guilds and unions representing talent, such as the American Federation of Musicians (AF of M) (212-869-1330) and the American Federation of Television and Radio Artists (AFTRA) (213-461-8111) require that you pay *reuse* (or new use) fees to the original singers, players, orchestra members, and so on who made the original recording. Even if the underlying music is in the public domain, if a piece was performed by a working member of the AF of M, you will be required to pay union scale to each musician. Music recorded overseas may be exempt from reuse fees.

8.2.1.5 Restrictions on Rights

Some songwriting and recording contracts may contain a clause that gives the composer or artist the right of approval over how a given song or performance can be used. The concern here is that the goodwill associated with the song will be damaged if it is used in the wrong context. Songwriters, for example, are very concerned about song parodies and how parodies will affect the earning power of the underlying composition, to say nothing of their reputation. Therefore, before you alter or adapt a musical work, or you change its basic melody or character, get permission from the copyright owner.

8.2.2   Film and TV Clips

Most film- and TV-clip licenses require releases from actors (including stunt people) featured in the clip, as well as from the owner of the film or TV show. This is because an individual's right of publicity is separate from the copyright in the underlying clip. For motion-picture clips, contact the Screen

Actors Guild (SAG) (213-954-1600), which will help you locate the performer's agent. For television clips, contact AFTRA (213-461-8111). Because the right of publicity protects voices as well as images, the rights to use the voices of principal actors, including narrators, must also be cleared.

If a film clip contains music, you must obtain permission from the musicians and from the composer separately. Consents (and reuse fees) are also required from the other creators, including writers, directors, and the various talent guilds, some of which may have special interactive-media agreements. Always inquire whether rights are available on a worldwide basis—if so needed—and whether material featuring "talent" requires additional clearances.

Special attention should also be paid to how your work depicts recognizable places, products, logos, and living people. Your best insurance against a claim of trademark infringement, libel, or invasion of privacy is a signed release or consent form. Keep in mind that minors cannot give consent, but their legal guardians can (see Chapter 10, "How to Minimize Libel Claims").

Most film clips are licensed on the basis of how much footage you need and how you plan to use the material, with a set minimum fee. All costs—including research, screening, duplication, and shipping—are usually borne by the person clearing the rights. If you've never cleared stock film footage, be aware that there are screening charges, typically between $25 and $35 per hour, plus research fees, which currently hover in the $50 to $65 per hour range. In addition, laboratory and tape-transfer fees are typically charged to the client. In trying to minimize costs, bear in mind that a good source of public domain footage is the National Archives in Washington, DC (202-501-5400), as well as various other agencies of the U.S. government.

8.2.3   Photos and Other Artwork

Many producers turn to stock houses for still pictures. Stock houses offer an alternative to commissioning works on a work for hire basis. With a stock house, you can purchase the use of an image that already exists. Stock houses tend to specialize in particular genres of images (e.g., sports, animals, or people.) Most charge flat rates. A few work on a royalty basis, although that is the exception, not the rule. Most stock agencies will license works for multimedia use, although some individual photographers may not.

If you intend to use a photographic reproduction of a work of art, up to three clearances may be involved. For example, a photograph taken directly from an original painting must be cleared with the artist or with the artist's estate if the painting is still in copyright. Because you will be reproducing from a color transparency or a digitized slide, you must also secure rights from the photographer who owns the copyright in the transparency. Even if the underlying work, or original visual image, is in the public domain, the original transparency must be cleared. Bear in mind that obtaining rights from one of the rights holders does not automatically give you permission to use the work. Each layer of rights may have to be cleared separately. If acquiring a transparency from a museum or gallery, ask whether the museum or gallery has the authority to license you the rights in both the underlying work and the transparency.

As we discuss in depth in Chapter 11, "Basics of Publicity and Privacy," individuals are entitled to certain rights of publicity and privacy. If a person is pictured in a work of art, these rights may apply. Under the right of publicity, individuals are entitled to control the commercial exploitation of their images. Unless there is a legitimate editorial reason (e.g., a photograph of Elizabeth Taylor used in an unauthorized CD-ROM biography), consent is generally required to use the person's image.

Due to the ease with which digital images can be copied and altered, some rights holders will not allow you to manipulate their images, either by cropping or by digital alteration. Similarly, some permission agreements require that the image will not be downloaded, or that the image will be kept at a resolution of 72 dots per inch (dpi) or less.

8.2.4   Cartoon Characters

Cartoon characters and other visual characters may be protected under the dual theories of copyright and trademark law. Character rights are jealously guarded by their owners, and the fees charged are usually very high. Most well-known entertainment characters are licensed by syndicates or licensing agents. Start with the studio or syndicate itself, the name of which should be listed next to the copyright (or trademark) notice. However, if you want to locate a particular cartoonist, you might start with the Motion Picture Screen Cartoonists Union (818-766-7151) or the National Cartoonists Society (212-627-1550).

8.2.5   Text

While sound and images may provide the allure, text is often the engine that drives a successful multimedia product. Text can be used in either of two ways: (1) as supplemental content, incorporated in whole, or in part, in the multimedia work; or (2) in the form of a multimedia product based on one or more preexisting works. In copyright jargon, a work based on previous works is known as a derivative work. An example of a derivative work is a CD-ROM version, or adaptation, of a best-selling children's book. The right to make (and to allow others to make) derivative works belongs exclusively to the copyright owner. If you want to make a new multimedia version of a Dr. Seuss book, you will need a special kind of exclusive license or agreement, which is beyond the scope of this book.

The major problem you'll encounter in licensing text for multimedia use is in determining who owns the actual right to license you the multimedia (or "electronic") rights. Older publishing agreements are often vague on the subject of new technology rights, making rights clearance a complex process. With newer publishing agreements, the party who controls electronic rights (i.e., the author or the publisher) is a matter of negotiation. Keep in mind that even if the publisher controls electronic rights, the author may have a right of approval over the use of his or her work.

If you want permission to reprint material from a book, seek out the hardcover, not the paperback, publisher. If the publisher doesn't control electronic rights, the publisher will refer you to the author, or the author's literary agent, who will.

If you choose to reproduce material that has appeared in a magazine or other type of periodical, you should proceed with caution. If the article was written by a staff reporter, the periodical will control the copyright, including the right to grant permission, as a work for hire. If the article was written by a freelancer, the periodical probably received *one-time rights*, which means the author controls reprint rights. As a rule, a newspaper or other periodical cannot grant permission to use material provided by freelancers, wire services, syndicates, and other services.

Part Two

The Libel Handbook

9

Basics of Libel Law

The law of defamation (which encompasses both written and oral statements) protects individuals from attacks on their reputations. The basic goal of defamation law is to provide a financial remedy for people who have been personally attacked and who have suffered embarrassment or damage to their reputations. *Libel*, which involves the publication of written defamatory material, can occur through the use of an inaccurate quotation, the improper use of legal terminology, a false statement, a miscaptioned photograph, or the omission of pertinent facts. Both nonfiction and fiction works can be defamatory. Consider these examples:

- Novelist Gwen Davis Mitchell set out to write a novel about the leisure class. She attended a "nude marathon encounter group therapy session" conducted by a licensed clinical psychologist, Dr. Paul Bindrim, Ph.D., as part of her research. In her book she described a nude encounter marathon session led by a fictitious therapist named Dr. Simon Herford, M.D. The fictional character was described as a domineering man who used obscenities and vulgar speech and who upset his patients. There were several dissimilarities between the real Dr. Bindrim and the fictional Dr. Herford, and most of the incidents portrayed in the book were fictional. Dr. Bindrim sued Gwen Mitchell for libel, and the jury, which believed there were sufficient similarities between the real and the fictional doctors, awarded Dr. Bindrim $75,000. The award was upheld on appeal.
- The *National Enquirer*, as part of its gossip column, printed a very brief story about comedienne Carol Burnett that consisted of four

sentences under the headline "Carol Burnett and Henry K. in Row." The article stated that Carol Burnett had a loud argument with Henry Kissinger in a Washington restaurant and said that she accidentally knocked over a glass of wine onto another diner. Burnett sued the *National Enquirer,* claiming that the article was false and that it implied that she was intoxicated and that all of the facts stated in the article were false. The jury awarded damages of $300,000 and punitive damages of $1.3 million, which were later lowered on appeal to a total award of $200,000.

9.1   Libel Defined

A libelous statement is a false statement of fact that injures or harms the reputation of a living person or an existing business. You cannot libel the dead. For a statement to be libelous, it must have been published and read by someone other than the person who was defamed. In addition, the defendant (i.e., the author, the publisher, or both) must have published the statement with the requisite degree of fault. For example, whether the injured party is a public official or private individual is crucial to determining liability (see Section 9.6). In certain circumstances, the plaintiff must also prove that he or she suffered economic harm.

The best defense to libel is verifiable truth, which means that the easiest way to steer clear of litigation is to practice good journalism. Check and recheck your sources. A true statement can't be libelous.

Bear in mind that a plaintiff does not have to show that the entire work is defamatory—just a single defamatory sentence, or improperly captioned photograph, can be enough.

9.1.1   What Is a Defamatory Statement?

The classic definition of a *defamatory statement* is words that "tend to expose one to public hatred, shame, obloquy, contumely, odium, contempt, ridicule, aversion, ostracism, degradation or disgrace, or to induce an evil opinion of one in the minds of right-thinking persons, and to deprive one of their confidence and friendly intercourse in society." In addition to this broad list, statements that tend to disparage a person in her or his office, profession, career, or trade are also considered defamatory.

9.1.2   Libel Per Se

When a written statement is defamatory on its face—that is, the statement contains all of the elements necessary to constitute defamation without any other information—it is considered to be *libel per se*. One example of a libel per se is the statement, "John Doe is a dishonest person who has been convicted of tax fraud"—assuming, that is, that John Doe is not a dishonest person and has never been convicted of tax fraud. The statement clearly identifies John Doe and makes a defamatory statement about him that would lower his reputation for honesty to any person who read the statement. Obviously, any person who read the statement would be quite hesitant to extend credit to John Doe.

9.1.3   Libel by Implication

A written statement that is not defamatory on its face may still be libelous if it implies false facts. The legal term for a statement that is libelous by implication is *libel per quod*. A classic example of libel by implication is the publication in a newspaper of a marriage notice stating that John Doe married Jane Doe, when the groom is misidentified and is already married. The publication of the marriage notice itself is not defamatory, because it doesn't appear on its face to make any defamatory statements to an ordinary reader of the newspaper. However, the knowledge in the community that the purported groom is already married makes the publication libelous.

9.2   *Name-Calling and Opinion*

Because a libelous statement must contain or imply a statement of fact, courts have held that statements of opinion and mere name-calling are not defamatory under many circumstances. However, if a statement of opinion can be reasonably construed to imply some false underlying facts, then even an opinion may give rise to a defamation lawsuit. The law recognizes that an otherwise defamatory statement should not be shielded from liability merely because the speaker frames the statement with words such as "in my opinion" or "it is my belief." Similarly, while name-calling is tolerated by the law, statements that can be interpreted as factual in nature, or as reasonably implying facts, can give rise to a defamation lawsuit, even if the facts are implied through innuendo. The use of opinion as a defense is described in more detail in Section 9.12.2.

9.3   There Is No Uniform Law of Libel in the United States

Defamation is a creature of state law. There is no federal libel law. However, layered on top of the state law tort of libel is the First Amendment, which protects freedom of expression and guarantees that topics of public interest can be freely and openly discussed. Due to First Amendment considerations, the test for liability depends on whether the person suing is a public or private figure, or whether the defamatory statement concerns a matter of public or private interest.

In the United States alone, there are 51 different libel laws (including the District of Columbia). Authors and publishers need to take into account all 51 different laws, not to mention the laws of other countries where their work will probably be distributed. Therefore, the following are general libel guidelines. The key test in all states, however, is whether the statement injures the subject's reputation.

9.4   The Types of Things That Can Be Defamatory

Any printed or communicated matter or any verbal statement can be defamatory. A photograph (if altered or if published along with an unrelated story), a headline, an advertisement, a cartoon, or even a poem or short article can defame someone if it is distributed to or read by a third person and it conveys a false and defamatory statement of fact that causes damages. Even quoting a person inaccurately in a way that would damage his or her reputation can be defamatory. Furthermore, communication to a third party by any means or technology can constitute publication for purposes of defamation law. Therefore, electronic publications, as well as print publications, can constitute libel.

9.5   The Elements of a Defamation Case

Technically, a plaintiff must prove four main elements in order to make a case of defamation: (1) falseness, (2) defamatory meaning, (3) identification of the plaintiff, and (4) publication. If a plaintiff makes his or her case, the burden shifts to the libel defendant to prove that the defendant is entitled to one of the defenses listed in Section 9.12.

9.5.1   The First Factor: A False Statement of Fact

To be libelous, a statement must be false. Truth is a complete defense to libel. If the statement is true, or substantially true, it is not defamatory. However, in cases involving private individuals or involving matters that are *not* of public concern, the person bringing the lawsuit does not have to prove that the statement was false. Instead, in these cases, the burden ordinarily falls on the author or publisher to prove the truth of the statement as an affirmative defense. A different rule applies when the plaintiff is a public figure or a public official or when the statement involves a matter of public concern. In these cases, as discussed in Section 9.6, the plaintiff must prove not only that the statement made about him or her was false, but also that the statement was published with knowledge of its falsity or with reckless disregard as to whether or not it was true. Caution is therefore urged when writing about private individuals involved in a nonpublic controversy. Since the author must prove the truth as an affirmative defense in these cases, defending a lawsuit can be very expensive.

9.5.2   The Second Factor: Defamatory Meaning

The statement must also cause or be likely to cause injury to someone's reputation. Remember, a defamatory statement tends to injure someone's reputation; tends to expose someone to public hatred, contempt, ridicule, disgrace, or embarrassment; or tends to disparage a person in his or her office, profession, career, or trade. While any statement could potentially cause such injury and therefore be considered defamatory, a few categories of statements are almost always defamatory.

These categories include statements in which a person is charged with the commission of a crime or of criminal conduct; statements in which a person is accused of having an infectious or loathsome disease; statements affecting a person in his or her political office, profession, or business; statements that attribute poverty or uncreditworthiness; statements accusing someone of being left out of a will or of disinheriting someone; statements affecting a person's ownership or interest in land or real estate; and statements implying that a person is unchaste or promiscuous.

These categories are not exclusive. Any other false statement of fact can also be potentially defamatory if it is false and it causes some type of harm to reputation or pecuniary damage.

9.5.3   The Third Factor: Statements "Of and Concerning" the Plaintiff

The defamatory statement must be about the plaintiff. In legal jargon, the plaintiff must prove that the statement is "of and concerning" the person claiming to be defamed. Bear in mind that the plaintiff need not be mentioned by name. The reference may be indirect. Further, the author need not intend to identify the plaintiff. The law requires only that an ordinary and reasonable person who knew the plaintiff and who read the statement must be able to identify the plaintiff as the subject of the statement. The identification can arise from facts contained in the statement or from other facts known by the reader or from separate sources.

There is a saying in defamation law that "it's not who was meant, but who is hit." It doesn't matter whether an author misidentifies the subject of a defamatory statement. Anyone who is reasonably identified by the publication can sue for defamation.

9.5.4   The Fourth Factor: Publication or Republication

The last factor requires that the allegedly defamatory statement be published or disseminated to a third party. In the law of libel, the word *publication* requires only that the statement be made to, or overheard by, at least one person other than the person defamed. Therefore, merely sending a single copy of a book to one person other than the defamed person constitutes publication.

Any republication of the statement (by the third party receiving it or by a publisher) is itself defamatory and can lead to liability for the person republishing or disseminating the statement. Thus, someone who publishes an unprivileged defamatory remark by someone else is subject to liability even though the statement is properly attributed to its source.

Tip	Whoever publishes, repeats, or republishes a libelous statement can be held legally responsible. Don't assume that you cannot be liable for defamation just because the statement has already been published by someone else. One who repeats a libelous statement may be just as liable as if he or she had originated it.

9.6   Differentiation between Private Citizens and Public Officials and Figures

The level of fault needed to prove libel depends on who the plaintiff, or person suing, is. In the law of defamation, the identity of the person bringing the lawsuit has a significant effect on the liability of the defendant. This is due to the fact that in the United States, private citizens are entitled to broader protection than are public figures and government officials. In the landmark case of *New York Times v. Sullivan*, 376 U.S. 254 (1964), the U.S. Supreme Court acknowledged that the First Amendment prohibits a public official from recovering damages from a defamatory falsehood relating to his or her official conduct unless he or she proves that the statement was made with actual malice. *Actual malice* means with knowledge that it was false or with reckless disregard of whether it was true or false.

What this means is that the press—including book publishers—enjoy broad protection when they cover matters of general public interest relating to public officials. For instance, a public official cannot collect damages even if the statement about his or her official conduct is false, unless the official proves that the statement was made with actual malice.

TIP Sitting on top of state-law defamation is the First Amendment, which protects freedom of expression and guarantees that issues relating to public concern may be freely and openly debated. Therefore, in deference to the First Amendment, writers and publishers are held to a lower standard of care when writing about public officials and public figures. That standard is known as the "actual malice" standard.

9.6.1   Who Are Public Officials?

Public officials are persons who have substantial responsibility for governmental affairs or policies. They include most public servants, including politicians and others holding positions in government, whether on the local, state, or federal level, and whether elected or appointed. Public officials also generally include candidates for elective office, public employees, police and other law-enforcement officers and officials, and public-school teachers and coaches. Even low-level police officers and county social workers have been found by some courts to be public officials. Most other public employees are not considered to be public officials unless they have policymaking authority, in which case they might be considered public officials.

9.6.2   Who Are Public Figures?

In later cases, the Supreme Court extended the actual malice rule, which it defined in the *New York Times v. Sullivan* case, to apply not only to public officials but also to public figures as well. The Supreme Court reasoned that when celebrities and other public figures voluntarily seek the public spotlight, they open themselves up to public criticism and comment. Therefore, they are held to the same standard as public officials, and they must likewise prove actual malice in order to win a libel lawsuit.

There are two types of public figures: (1) all-purpose public figures, and (2) limited purpose public figures. *All-purpose public figures* are people who are well known and have access to the press. All-purpose public figures include celebrities, professional athletes, and others who are in the public spotlight or who have become household names. When people who are not well-known personalities thrust themselves into the forefront of a particular public controversy in order to influence its outcome, then they may be considered *limited purpose public figures* for the purposes of that particular public controversy.

For example, an individual who takes a leading position in a campaign to recall a mayor or other local official may become a limited purpose public figure for the purpose of that controversy. Likewise, a witness in a controversial or high-profile trial may become a limited purpose public figure as a result of the publicity related to the trial. Similarly, anyone who publishes a book usually becomes a limited purpose public figure for the purpose of what he or she has written about.

9.6.3   How to Tell If Someone Is a Limited Purpose
Public Figure

Just because a person receives a lot of publicity does not mean that he or she is necessarily a public figure, even for a limited purpose. If people have not voluntarily thrust themselves into the vortex of a public issue in order to influence its outcome and have not voluntarily sought out the public's attention, they might not be public figures, even for a limited purpose.

To find out if someone is a limited purpose public figure, it is helpful to ask the following questions:

- Is there a public controversy?
- If so, did the person thrust himself or herself to the forefront of that controversy?

- Is the alleged defamatory remark germane to the person's participation in that public controversy?

Unfortunately, there are no hard-and-fast rules to determine who is a limited purpose public figure. People who are classified as private figures, *not* limited purpose public figures, include (1) a prominent socialite involved in a divorce from her wealthy husband; (2) a research scientist held up to ridicule by a U.S. senator for using public grants for unorthodox research; and (3) a journalist, misidentified in a photograph as the person who assassinated Robert F. Kennedy.

9.7   Differentiation between Public and Private Subject Matter

In addition to differentiating between public and private plaintiffs, the law of defamation also differentiates between public and private subject matter. This is also due to the constitutional rights of citizens and the press to discuss matters of public concern. Therefore, when a defamatory statement involves a matter of public controversy, the plaintiff is again required to bear the burden of proving that the author or publisher acted with some degree of fault in order to recover damages in a lawsuit.

Keep in mind that the degree of fault to be proven depends, once again, on who the plaintiff is. If the plaintiff is a public figure or a public official, he or she must prove "actual malice." However, even when the statement involves a matter of public controversy, if the plaintiff is a private, non-public person, the degree of fault required to win a libel lawsuit may be nothing more than negligence. That means that the plaintiff in these cases is only required to prove that the author acted carelessly, even if he or she didn't know that the statement was false.

9.7.1   What Are Public Controversies?

Public controversies are disputes that receive public attention because their ramifications will affect people who are not direct participants. These are disputes that will have some effect on the public at large, such as political events and elections, criminal trials, and governmental proceedings. There must be a specific issue that is actually being discussed by the public or at least by a significant number of people.

In addition, the controversy must precede the publication of the allegedly defamatory statement. Authors and publishers charged with defamation cannot create their own defense by making the subject matter of the defamatory statement a public figure or making the matter a public controversy after the fact.

9.7.2   What Degree of Fault Is Necessary?

Although plaintiffs are usually required to prove that the publisher or author acted with some degree of fault when the statement involves a matter of public controversy, the level of proof varies from state to state. In most states, the plaintiff must prove that the author and the publisher were at least grossly negligent. Many states have even adopted an actual malice requirement when dealing with speech on matters of public concern.

9.7.3   What Constitutes Actual Malice?

Actual malice, which is the standard by which defendants in libel suits brought by public officials and public figures are measured, means that the author or publisher acted with "knowledge of falsity or with reckless disregard for the truth." Therefore, courts look at the state of mind of, and the information available to, the author or publisher. In order to act with actual malice, the author or the publisher must have known that the statement was false or must have entertained serious doubts as to its truth or accuracy at the time it was made.

An author's reliance on a single uncorroborated source for information concerning a public figure or official, provided that source is a reputable source, does not by itself suggest actual malice. For example, because *The New York Times* is considered a reliable source, basing one's conclusions on an article in the "newspaper of record" without further investigation does not alone suggest actual malice. Similarly, a publisher may rely on an author's credentials to avoid actual malice. If an author or a publisher has no reason to believe that information from a reputable source was inaccurate, there is no duty to conduct a further investigation. Of course, if the author (or publisher) doubts the reliability of a source, or knows the source is biased, actual malice may be found.

A publisher's or an author's gross departure from journalistic practices may also be considered evidence of actual malice. Similarly, if a publisher intentionally alters quotations or information to the extent that a material change in the meaning is conveyed by the altered statement, the publisher may be liable for defamation under the actual malice standard.

Mere factual inaccuracies, inconsistencies in an article, sloppy reporting, sloppy investigation, and errors of interpretation do not constitute actual malice, although they may constitute negligence, which can give rise to liability when dealing with private individuals who are not public figures. However, negligence is not sufficient to constitute actual malice.

Because the actual malice standard requires an author and a publisher to act in good faith and with reasonable diligence, the duty of care correlates to the amount of time an author has to write the work. For example, an author who spends years researching a biography is generally expected to spend more time researching and verifying facts than is an investigative reporter on a tight deadline for a daily newspaper. As a general rule, the more time you have available to write and research, the more careful you have to be.

9.7.4   What Happens When the Statement Is about a Private Person and Does Not Involve a Matter of Public Concern?

When the plaintiff is a private citizen and the subject matter is purely of private concern, the publisher and the author can be liable for damages for merely negligently publishing a false statement. In these cases, sloppy investigation or sloppy reporting can give rise to liability. While the specific level of proof varies from state to state, the plaintiff need not prove that the author or the publisher acted recklessly or intentionally. Thus, authors and publishers are open to greater liability in cases where private individuals are defamed and the subject matter of the statement is not of public concern.

9.8   Entities That Can Be Defamed

There are several categories of entities that can be defamed, including living persons and existing businesses, as well as small, identifiable groups.

9.8.1   Living Persons and Businesses

Generally, any living person can be defamed. However, individuals are not the only ones capable of being defamed. In fact, companies, corporations, partnerships, and businesses can also be defamed. Therefore, authors must be wary of unflattering and potentially embarrassing or harmful statements made about living persons, companies, and even products (see Section 9.9). However, just as a dead person cannot sue for defamation, a defunct corporation or business is also generally prohibited from maintaining a defamation lawsuit.

Tip	While dead people cannot be defamed, if a person is defamed when alive, in most cases, the estate will have the right to bring a lawsuit on the person's behalf. Similarly, if a person starts a defamation lawsuit while alive and dies while the case is pending, the plaintiff's estate will usually be allowed to continue the lawsuit after the plaintiff's death.

9.8.2 Small Identifiable Groups

In addition, members of small and identifiable groups that are defamed (usually groups of 25 people or less) can also bring lawsuits in their own names as members of the defamed group. When dealing with statements made about groups of people, the test is generally whether any single member of the group could reasonably claim to have been identified or referred to by the statement.

Tip	While a rule of thumb limits lawsuits to members of groups of 25 or less, on occasion, members of groups consisting of more than 25 individuals have been allowed by the courts. In one case, a member of a football team with more than 60 members was allowed to maintain a libel claim against a publisher who accused the entire team of using amphetamines.

9.9 Product Disparagement

Product disparagement, also known as "trade libel," occurs when a defamatory statement is made about a product. While the law varies from state to state, ordinarily product disparagement occurs when a false statement of fact is published about a manufacturer's product, and the author or publisher either knew that the statement was false or intended for the statement to harm the manufacturer's pecuniary interests. Product disparagement is often more difficult to prove than defamation. In fact, in some states, the plaintiff bears the burden of proving both that the defendant knew that the statement was false and that the defendant intended to harm the plaintiff's financial interests. Many states also require the plaintiff to prove that the plaintiff actually incurred out-of-pocket financial damages resulting from the disparaging statement.

Damaging statements about a product may constitute trade disparagement even if the statements do not constitute defamation against the manufacturer. However, a statement discrediting a person's or a company's personal business reputation, as well as the reputation or quality of the goods or products, may give rise to both a product disparagement claim and a defamation claim.

9.10   Types of Damages Available for Defamation

Libel plaintiffs are generally allowed to receive monetary damages from authors and publishers who publish defamatory works. Once plaintiffs demonstrate that they have suffered some damages, there are several remedies available, as follows: special damages, actual damages, punitive damages, and attorneys' fees and court costs.

9.10.1   Special Damages

Courts will award compensation for actual out-of-pocket losses suffered by the plaintiff as a result of the defamatory statement, including costs incurred as a result of rehabilitating the plaintiff's reputation or defending against claims made by people who read the defamatory statement. These damages for out-of-pocket losses and financial damages are commonly referred to as "special damages" in defamation law. The special damages award may also include interest from the date of the loss until the date the judgment is awarded.

9.10.2   Actual Damages

Courts will also often award plaintiffs compensation for injury and harm caused by the defamatory statement, including compensation for humiliation, embarrassment, and mental anguish and suffering. These damages for the personal injury and anxiety caused by the defamatory statement are commonly referred to as "actual damages."

9.10.3   Punitive Damages

Where the plaintiff can prove that the person who made the defamatory statement acted with *actual malice*—meaning that the person knew or had reason to know that the statement was false or otherwise acted with recklessness as to the truth or falsity of the statement—the plaintiff can be awarded punitive damages. Punitive damages are designed to punish the defendant for his or her intentional or reckless actions and indifference to the plaintiff's rights and feelings. The amount of punitive damages, if any, is strictly up to the jury or the court, provided that the damage award is not grossly excessive.

When dealing with claims of defamation against the press, courts are also wary that substantial punitive damage awards can have a chilling effect on the press by encouraging self-censorship. Therefore, many states discourage punitive damages in defamation cases.

9.10.4   Attorneys' Fees and Court Costs

If plaintiffs are successful in their defamation actions, the court may make the defendants reimburse the plaintiffs for all of their court costs and attorneys' fees. Often, the court costs and legal fees far outweigh the compensatory or punitive damage awards granted to the plaintiffs. It is very possible that a plaintiff could win a libel award of one dollar, representing the actual damages, but could also win an award requiring the defendant to pay the plaintiff's legal fees and court costs, which could total tens of thousands of dollars. Therefore, even when plaintiffs cannot prove substantial monetary damages but nevertheless have a case for defamation, defendants frequently settle the cases quickly in order to avoid having to pay the plaintiffs' legal fees.

9.11   Retraction of a Libelous Statement

Many state laws allow newspaper and magazine publishers to limit their liability for defamation by publishing a retraction if requested by the person alleging to have been libeled. As a general rule, these retraction statutes do not apply to book publishers. Therefore, only magazine and newspaper publishers can take advantage of them. While publication of a retraction or corrective advertising can help to appease someone who has been defamed and can help avoid a lawsuit, it is not generally recommended for book publishers. In fact, book publishers should always check with an experienced publishing attorney before attempting to publish a retraction, clarification, or correction, because such actions could serve as an admission that the statement was false and can then lead to liability. Be aware, however, that the time within which a publisher may issue a retraction to avoid liability may be very limited (48 hours in some states). Therefore, act promptly if you receive a complaint or letter claiming a passage is defamatory and untrue.

9.12   Defenses to a Claim of Defamation

Several defenses (and privileges) can be raised by authors and publishers in response to claims of defamation, although the best defense is always to be careful when publishing statements of fact about others. Nevertheless, following are discussions of some of the defenses available to defendants in libel lawsuits.

9.12.1   Truth

Truth is a complete defense to libel in most states. Some states require that the truthful, but defamatory, statement be published without bad intent. As a rule, if there is no *false* statement of fact, then there is no libel. Indeed, the statement need not even be *entirely* true or accurate: substantial truth is sufficient. Minor inaccuracies will be tolerated under defamation law; as long as the "gist" or the "sting" of the accusation is true, the statement will not be considered to be false. Because the law requires the gist of the statement to be true, if facts are published in a way that creates a false impression or false implication, the statement may be libelous. In these cases, where a false implication is created (either because the facts were juxtaposed or some material facts were omitted), the passage will be libelous even though the individual facts were technically true.

For example, suppose that Jan Criminal sues Lee Author because Lee Author claimed in Lee's book that Jan Criminal had been convicted of robbing two banks. The gist or sting of the allegation is that Jan Criminal is a bank robber. If it turns out that Jan Criminal had been convicted of robbing just one bank, not two, the gist of the statement is still true and accurate. In that case, the mere inaccuracy in the number of banks robbed probably will not defeat Lee Author's defense of truth.

Remember, when truth is the defense, the burden rests on the author and the publisher to prove it. Obviously, this means that defending a lawsuit with the defense of truth can be very expensive and time-consuming and subject to all of the uncertainties that are inherent in a lawsuit.

Therefore, authors and publishers should always be prepared to prove the truth of the statements they publish. This includes keeping detailed notes and records to substantiate your statements. While being able to prove the truth will not prevent lawsuits, in many cases the knowledge that the statement is true will discourage the agitated person from filing suit.

Finally, keep in mind that there is a vast difference between *knowing* the truth and *proving* the truth.

> **TIP**   It is imperative that authors save and catalog all notes and sources for their works so that they will be able to locate the source material in the event of a lawsuit. This material may help to establish truth, show credibility, or demonstrate the author's professionalism.

9.12.2   Opinion

As discussed briefly in Section 9.2, statements of opinion are not defamatory because they do not contain a false statement of fact. However, if an opinion implies a false statement of fact, it can be defamatory. Where an author reveals all of the underlying facts on which an opinion is based and makes that opinion depend solely on those facts without implying the existence of other underlying facts, the statement will be considered opinion. Because a statement of opinion cannot be provable as true or false, it is not defamatory. However, if the facts that are disclosed and on which the opinion is based are false and defamatory, the author can be liable for defamation as a result of publishing those false facts.

If a statement implies other facts than those disclosed, you cannot insulate yourself from liability by merely couching the statement in terms such as "in my opinion" or "my opinion is." After all, the statement "In my opinion, Smith is a liar" can cause as much damage as (if not more than) the statement "Smith is a liar." When evaluating whether a statement is an opinion or a fact, courts will scrutinize the statement in question to determine whether it is objective or subjective in nature and whether it could reasonably imply a verifiable false statement of fact. Context also plays a role. For instance, the statement "In my opinion, Dale is a liar"—standing alone—is potentially libelous because it could lead to the conclusion that the writer had undisclosed facts that justified the statement. However, if someone writes "Dale looks like she's 35, but she told me she's only 25. I think she lied about her age," obviously the writer did not actually know whether Dale lied or not. The statement is merely a guess, or conjecture. Of course, if the facts the opinion was based on are incorrect, or incomplete, there may still be a basis for a libel claim. Obviously, statements made in a biographical work are more likely to be interpreted as factual in nature than are those contained in a work of historical fiction.

9.12.3   Reviews and Critiques

Restaurant reviews and other critical reviews are more likely to be understood as expressing the reviewer's personal opinions and not objective fact. Therefore, in most cases, a critic's bad review or poor opinion of a restaurant, play, or film is shielded from defamation claims as protected opinion, which does not involve an objective reporting of fact. However, many courts will rule that if a review or critique is made in bad faith or maliciously, and it does not represent the critic's honest opinion, the review may not be protected from defamation claims.

9.12.4   Name-Calling

Name-calling has a legal name for purposes of libel law. It is called "rhetorical hyperbole." Technically, any type of verbal abuse or imaginative speech can qualify as rhetorical hyperbole. Like opinion, these types of statements do not contain false statements of facts. Simply calling someone a "jerk," "traitor," "phony," or "loser" or referring to someone as "sleazy" is not defamatory because these terms are too vague to be objectively false. However, if you say someone is a "traitor because . . . ," whether the statement is libelous or not will depend on what you insert after the word "because."

Fortunately, courts tolerate some degree of undignified name-calling. In one case, a court held that calling a real estate developer's negotiation position "blackmail" was the type of name-calling that did not constitute libel. The court reasoned that the readers would understand that the word "blackmail," in context, was used in a loose, figurative way to suggest that the plaintiff was a tough negotiator. In short, under libel law you can be insulting, provided your statements are too vague to be proven false.

9.12.5   Statements Not "Of and Concerning" the Plaintiff

The law requires that a defamatory statement must reasonably identify a person in order to give rise to a lawsuit. Therefore, a valid defense can be made by proving that the statement in question does not reasonably identify the plaintiff. Unfortunately for authors and publishers, the rule is one of reason. The law does not require the statement to name the plaintiff personally. The law only requires that any person who knows the plaintiff and who read or heard the statement would reasonably be able to identify the statement to be about or to describe the plaintiff. The context or other disclosed information can be used to help identify the actual subject. As discussed in Section 9.13, even a fictional work can be defamatory if a real person can reasonably be identified as the story's character.

9.12.6   Consent

Consent is always an absolute defense. Any person can give another person permission to defame him or her. Once the subject of the statement has consented to publication of the statement, the author and the publisher can publish the statement without liability. When authors obtain releases from subjects described in their works, the release serves as a consent and, thus, an absolute defense to a libel claim. However, authors need to be wary, because the consent may be limited to a particular publication or to a particular statement. If an author or a publisher exceeds the scope of the consent given, the author and the publisher may be subject to liability. Just because a subject has given consent for an author to use a statement in one book or in one context doesn't mean that the author has the right to use that statement in another book or another context without liability.

Furthermore, consent can only be given by the actual subject of the statement or by the subject's legal guardian or agent. When obtaining a consent or a release, it is important to make sure that you obtain the consent from the subject or the subject's legal representative, or the consent may not be valid.

9.12.7   Privileged Statements

The aforementioned defenses are available to anyone being sued for libel. These defenses make a statement nonlibelous. However, there are other defenses called "privileges." *Privileges* technically do not make an otherwise defamatory statement nondefamatory; rather, they excuse the person making the defamatory statement from liability, based on public policy considerations. Privileges generally protect a person who makes a statement pursuant to a legal or moral duty.

There are two types of privileges: "absolute" and "conditional." An *absolute privilege* applies regardless of whether the person making the statement acts in good faith. *Conditional privileges* are conditioned on the good faith of the person making the statement. If the person making the statement, or republishing it, acts with ill will, hatred, or evil intentions, the conditional privilege will not apply.

Beware. Both absolute and conditional privileges can be overcome if the matters published are not a fair and accurate report of the proceedings.

9.12.7.1 Absolute Privileges

Absolute privileges serve to protect the legal and political process by protecting speech made during a judicial, legislative, or executive governmental proceeding.

1. *Judicial proceedings.* Generally, statements made by participants during the course of judicial proceedings in open court and during legislative proceedings are considered to be privileged and cannot be the basis for a defamation action. Statements made during judicial proceedings in open court are usually absolutely privileged, with exceptions in only a few states. The privilege extends both to statements made by judges, court officers, attorneys, and jurors, and to the testimony of parties and witnesses. The key is that they are made in open court and are reasonably related to the judicial proceedings.

    Because the purpose of the privilege is to encourage candor and openness in court proceedings and to allow the press to accurately report all statements made by persons involved in judicial proceedings, the privilege applies to all legal documents filed with the court—unless they are sealed and not open to the general public for inspection. The privilege also applies to statements made during depositions and pretrial conferences. The privilege does not apply, however, to statements made before judicial proceedings are commenced, or to statements made to the press or outside of a judicial context. Unfortunately, it is not always easy to determine when a judicial proceeding has commenced, or what constitutes a judicial context.

2. *Legislative proceedings.* Statements made during legislative proceedings are absolutely privileged, even if they later turn out to be wrong. This means that authors and publishers can accurately report statements made by members of Congress and state legislatures with immunity. This absolute privilege extends to members of Congress

and their staff members for activities related to the legislative process, including speeches and statements made on the floor of Congress, in committee meetings and hearings, and in committee reports. This privilege also extends to witnesses who testify at congressional hearings. This privilege does not extend, however, to statements made outside of legislative proceedings, such as statements made at press conferences, press releases, and statements made by members of Congress while not on the floor of either house.

Most state constitutions have a provision providing immunity for state legislators, and the common law of defamation also generally provides an absolute immunity for state legislative proceedings. Therefore, the same rules generally apply when dealing with statements made at state-level and local-level legislative proceedings.

3. *Executive absolute privilege.* An absolute privilege also serves to protect federal executive-branch members from liability for otherwise defamatory statements made while in office. The privilege extends to statements made by executive-branch members within the scope of their official duties. This allows them to speak freely and openly with respect to matters of public importance, without fear of legal repercussions. The majority of state laws generally provide for a similar absolute privilege for statements made by governors and state officials while acting within the scope of their duties. However, the law varies from state to state, and local law should be checked before relying on an absolute privilege at the state executive level. This privilege permits authors and publishers to accurately report and republish statements made by federal and state governmental officials without fear of being sued for defamation.

9.12.7.2 Conditional Privileges

Conditional privileges tend to protect writers and publishers where there is an important public interest at stake. These privileges are conditioned, however, on the writer's or publisher's good faith. A showing that the writer or publisher abused the privilege, acted in malice, desired to harm the subject, or otherwise acted in bad faith will override the privilege and open the author and publisher to liability for defamation. Likewise, the privilege will also be defeated if there is evidence that the author or publisher did not believe that the statement was true or had serious reason to doubt the truth of the statement but published it anyway.

Among the types of conditional privileges are the following:

1. *Statements that protect the public interest.*   A conditional privilege applies to statements that reasonably serve to protect an important public interest, such as statements concerning government employees and communications made to police officers and law-enforcement officials. This includes publication of police reports and telephone calls to police and fire departments.

2. *Accurate report of an official or public proceeding.*   Accurate reports of official or public proceedings are also subject to a conditional privilege. The privilege applies to republications of statements made as part of public proceedings, as long as the report is an accurate and full report or is a fair abridgement or summary of the proceeding reported. This means that authors can accurately reprint statements made during public meetings.

3. *The right to reply.*   Authors and publishers are generally permitted to publish statements in reply to claims against them. As an example, if an author is accused of publishing a defamatory statement, the author may respond to those allegations by publishing the facts known to him or her and other bases for the statements without further liability.

9.13   The Law of Libel and Fictional Works

Just because a literary work based on real events or real people has been disguised as a fictional work does not mean that it cannot give rise to a lawsuit for defamation. In fact, fictional works may give rise to an action for defamation if, despite a writer's attempts to disguise the identity of an actual person, a reasonable reader could still identify the subject, and the work could be reasonably understood as describing actual facts about the subject. This applies to companies as well as to individuals who are fictionalized. In fact, authors may even be liable when a fictional work accidentally describes a real person.

Tip   When fictionalizing a real story or real people, make sure you change all of the names, descriptions, and locations sufficiently so that no one, not even a friend of the person described, could link the real person with the fictional character. If you must base a fictional character on a living person, make certain the fictional aspects of the character are innocuous or clearly fictional.

9.13.1   Similarities with an Actual Person

As a general rule in *libel in fiction* cases, the plaintiff must prove that the similarities between the actual individual and the fictional character are so complete that the defamatory material becomes a plausible aspect of the real-life plaintiff or suggestive of the plaintiff in significant ways. Further, a reader's conclusion that the published material is about the plaintiff must be reasonable in light of the full context of the fictional work. Therefore, if the allegedly defamatory statement is not believable or plausible, there is no liability.

Because there is a presumption that all the material in a fictional work is untrue, the courts require the plaintiff to overcome this presumption by proving that the allegations are plausible. Therefore, the more fantastic or clearly impossible those fictional or dramatic elements are, the less likely the portrayal will be considered defamatory. As one court has put it, the plaintiff "must demonstrate that third parties apprehend the similarity between the real person and her [or his] literary cognate as something more than amusing coincidence or even conscious parallelism on a superficial basis. Rather it is required that the reasonable reader must rationally suspect that the [character described in the work] is in fact the plaintiff." In other words, "the description of the fictional character must be so closely akin to the real person claiming to be defamed that a reader of the book, knowing the real person, would have no difficulty linking the two."

CASE AND COMMENT

In *Bindrim v. Mitchell,* 92 Cal. App 3d 61 (Cal. App 2 Dist, 1979), Gwen Davis Mitchell, a best-selling author, wanted to write about a clinical psychologist, Paul Bindrim, Ph.D., in her book about women of the leisure class. Dr. Bindrim used what he called "Nude Marathons," a sort of group therapy, to help people shed their inhibitions about being nude. The author attempted to register in Dr. Bindrim's nude-therapy sessions, but he specifically told her that she could not register for the session if she intended to write about it. Deceptively, the author told Dr. Bindrim that she was attending the sessions solely for personal therapy. Moreover, the author signed a contract agreeing not to write about the sessions. However, the author later wrote a novel entitled *Touching,* depicting a nude encounter session in Southern California led by a person named "Dr. Simon Herford," who used foul language.

Dr. Bindrim sued Mitchell and her publisher for defamation, claiming that the book portrayed him inaccurately and in a defamatory way by describing him as "crude, aggressive and unprofessional." Mitchell claimed that the book was a work of fiction and that it did not describe

Dr. Bindrim, citing the fact that the character in the book was named "Simon Herford." In addition, she claimed that "Herford" did not look anything like Dr. Bindrim, and the book was clearly labeled a work of fiction. The court held that there were sufficient similarities between Dr. Bindrim and Simon Herford for a jury to find that the book was "of and concerning" Dr. Bindrim. Further, the novel closely described the actual events that occurred during Dr. Bindrim's nude marathon sessions, providing additional evidence that the book was about Dr. Bindrim.

The author could potentially have avoided liability by changing the true events sufficiently so that no participant in Dr. Bindrim's therapy session could have recognized the book as describing either Dr. Bindrim's sessions or Dr. Bindrim himself. The author also should not have signed a contract agreeing not to publish any accounts of the therapy session.

9.13.2   Nonfiction Novels and "Faction"

The involvement of a lawyer is recommended if you intend to mix fact and fiction in a story inspired by actual events, such as a "nonfiction novel." If a fictional story is based on actual events or people, and the fictionalization portrays an identifiable person in an unsavory light, make sure that the depiction conforms to the actual person and events and that you can prove the truth of each matter alleged. If not, your fictionalization may not be legally defensible. One way to do this is by indicating, line by line in the draft copy of your manuscript, the factual basis and original source for the material. You should not place a person in a worse light than the facts would otherwise suggest. If you portray a well-known public figure, the character should be incidental to the story and the portrayal unobjectionable. If the person is dead, he or she can figure more prominently in your story, because you cannot defame the dead. Also, be careful that composite characters do not accidentally identify living persons. First novels, which are often autobiographical, therefore, should be scrutinized carefully.

Finally, a "nonfiction novel," sometimes known as "faction," based on private incidents involving private figures, places you at extreme risk because of the right of private individuals to be left alone, and because private persons do not have to prove "actual malice" in libel suits.

9.13.3   If the Work Is Fictional, Include a Disclaimer

If the work is fictional, it is advisable to include a disclaimer stating that the work is fictional and is not based on any real people or events. While a disclaimer will not prevent a lawsuit (or even ensure that you will win one), it may provide some ammunition to help you defend a lawsuit. The inclusion of a disclaimer can help you to argue that the work was completely fictional and that no reasonable person would believe that it was based on an actual person, especially after reading the disclaimer. Even the use of the two simple words, "A Novel," as a subtitle on the jacket of a book may serve as an adequate disclaimer in some cases. Sample disclaimers are contained in Appendix D.

CHECKLIST: Libel

- ☐ Is the subject identifiable? Would a reader who knows the subject be able to identify him or her either from the contents of the work or through other information known by the reader?
- ☐ If the work is fiction, is it based on a real person or event, which is thinly disguised? If so, have all identifying features of actual persons been adequately changed or hidden to disguise their identity?
- ☐ Is the subject a living person or an existing organization, such as a corporation?
- ☐ Would the reader's opinion or estimation of the subject be changed after reading the work?
- ☐ Would the subject's reputation be negatively affected by the work, or would an average reader form a lower opinion of the subject after reading the work?
- ☐ Does the work state or imply any facts, or does it make statements, that may be interpreted to be facts about the subject? If so, have they all been verified to be true?
- ☐ Have any important facts been omitted?
- ☐ Do you have sufficient evidence to prove the truth of the statements and implications? Are your information sources reliable?
- ☐ Does the context of the statement imply any additional facts that are substantially false?
- ☐ Do all of the captions, headlines, chapter headings, and titles accurately reflect the content of the material they describe?
- ☐ If the story or accusation were about you, would you believe that the writer used good faith and took reasonable steps to verify the accuracy of the statement and to publish the truth based on the information available?
- ☐ Is the subject a public official or a public figure? If so, have you acted with actual malice (i.e., do you think the statement is false, or do you have serious doubts or questions as to whether it is true)?

☐   Is the subject matter of the statement a matter of public importance or legitimate public concern? If so, have you acted with actual malice (i.e., do you think the statement is false, or do you have serious doubts or questions as to whether it is true)?

☐   Have you obtained a release or a written permission from the subject?

10

How to Minimize Libel Claims

While none of us can completely insulate ourselves from lawsuits, there are several ways in which authors and publishers can reduce their risk of a libel lawsuit. This chapter provides a general, basic guide to help you locate potentially libelous passages in your work.

All authors should know how to perform a careful basic libel review of their manuscripts. While no prepublication review by a layperson can take the place of the advice of an experienced lawyer familiar with the intricacies of libel and privacy law, you can still often identify blatant problems and fix them before the work is published.

Unfortunately, the prepublication libel review process cannot be reduced to a simple checklist or a single set of rules because libel law varies from state to state, and no two written works are the same. Libel is a very fact-specific area of the law, and each project has its own legal issues. In fact, in some cases, the addition or omission of a comma or semicolon can make an otherwise innocuous statement a libelous one.

TIP ☞	When reviewing your manuscript for possible libel and related privacy claims, remember to review the entire manuscript, including the preface, the afterword, and even photo captions. Any part of the manuscript or the materials (e.g., advertising copy, jacket copy and artwork, press release) that accompany it can give rise to a lawsuit.

While the following tips can help you spot libel problems early on, they may not help an untrained eye find all of them. Be careful, and always seek professional advice if you think your work is at risk for a lawsuit.

10.1   Verify Facts and the Accuracy of Statements

Obviously, one of the best ways to avoid libel claims is to be careful and accurate when reporting facts and events. Double-check the accuracy of all statements made about any living person or any contemporary company, business entity, or product. Make sure that you have some way of verifying the truth and accuracy of everything you've written, just in case a claim is brought. If you have any doubts about the accuracy of a particular source, get independent corroboration. Check headlines, captions, book flaps, and promotional and publicity materials that might be defamatory, even if the underlying story or material is true. Also, try to describe the story fairly, and include all sides of the story. There is no substitute for exercising good judgment and good journalistic skills.

10.2   Document Your Research

Authors should keep detailed logs of calls made during their fact-checking process. It is also helpful to make contemporaneous notes documenting your investigative techniques. If you can't reach a party on the phone to confirm facts, write to him or her instead. In case of a libel suit, be prepared to produce notes, drafts, and copies of source materials, including newspaper stories and other written documents. Similarly, you should be able to produce copies of recorded interviews. Those interviews should be clearly labeled, listing the name of the interviewee, and the date, time, and place of the interview. Get the interviewee to acknowledge on the tape that the interview is being done with his or her knowledge and that he or she consents to its use in your work. Use footnotes to back up what you write. A footnoted copy of your manuscript should be kept in a safe place so you can locate the source of specific information, or quotes, concerning real people and actual events. Finally, hold researchers you hire to the same high journalistic standards you hold yourself. If feasible, get the researchers to indemnify you in the event their contributions are found libelous, or invasive of someone's publicity, or privacy, rights.

10.3   Obtain a Release Whenever Possible

Whenever it's possible and practical to do so, get a written interview release. This will help you avoid libel and other claims. Although no contact is airtight, and the validity of a release, like any other agreement, may be challenged, it is very difficult to have a release disregarded by a court. In most cases, an "irrevocable" release will be binding.

10.4   Recognize the Kinds of Works Most Likely to Invite Libel Claims

First novels, fictionalizations, and investigative reports are the three kinds of works most likely to be found libelous. Consequently, these types of works should receive careful libel reviews.

10.5   Recognize the People Most Likely to Sue

Recognize the people who are most likely to sue for defamation, and make sure that you give works involving these kinds of people a careful libel review. Usually, the people most likely to sue are the following:

1. *Professionals.*   Professionals include doctors, chiropractors, attorneys, accountants, and others who have the financial resources to commence and maintain a lawsuit and who depend on their reputation for their livelihood.

2. *Public figures.*   Public figures are celebrities and other people in the public spotlight who make money based on their appeal to general audiences and who are paid to sponsor or endorse products. Many times, even if the celebrity does not want to start a legal battle, the celebrity's manager or agent (faced with lost revenues due to the loss of endorsements resulting from the defamatory statement) will encourage the celebrity to file a lawsuit. Remember, in deference to the first amendment, writers and publishers are held to a lower standard of care when writing about public figures. That standard is known as "actual malice."

3. *People whose jobs depend on reputation.*   Others whose jobs depend on their reputation and integrity include teachers, coaches, school principals and deans, professors, and priests, rabbis, and other clerics. These people have a lot to lose if they are portrayed in a negative light, and they often have enough money to hire a lawyer and to maintain a legal battle.

4. *Litigious people.*   If they've sued others before because of unflattering statements, don't think they won't sue you!

5. *Business executives.* Like clerics and school principals, business executives generally rely on their reputations and have corporate legal departments at their disposal, as well as enough money to bring a lawsuit.

6. *Peripheral figures.* People who are not central or necessary to the story told but, rather, are incidental or peripheral characters may be described in an unflattering light. Often, these people are just ordinary, private people who are not involved in the story but whose reputations are affected by being mentioned in the story. They often suffer more damage than the integral characters, and in many states they only have to prove that the statements about them were published negligently. They don't have to prove that the author or publisher acted recklessly or knew of the falsity of the statement. This makes these people attractive clients to libel lawyers.

10.6 Watch Out for Red Flag Statements

It is important to always be on the lookout for the types of statements that commonly give rise to defamation actions. These are sometimes referred to as "red flags." These statements include accusations that someone:

- committed a crime
- acted immorally or unethically
- acted with professional incompetence or committed malpractice
- is financially irresponsible
- is involved with a disreputable group or organization

When making one of these accusations, it is important to double-check the accuracy of the statement and to make sure that you have evidence to back up your statement. Also, it is extremely important to use criminal law terminology accurately. For example, if someone has been arrested for a crime, it is defamatory to say that the person has been convicted, because an arrest does not necessarily mean that a person is guilty. If you are going to accuse someone of a crime, make sure that you can prove that the person either confessed or was convicted.

10.7 Change All Names, Places, and Descriptions

If your account is based on real events or real characters but is partly or wholly fictional, you can help to reduce the risk of a libel lawsuit by changing the names and descriptions of all the actual people and places. You must adequately alter the names of people and places and actual events to avoid describing any real people or events. You may even want to change the actual subject's sex to avoid any recognition of the true person's identity.

In order to defeat a libel lawsuit against a fictional work, you must change all names and descriptions of actual people, events, and places sufficiently that no reader would be able to recognize their true identities. In addition, even when actual names, events, and places are sufficiently altered to avoid any recognition, if the work contains an afterword, an acknowledgment, or any other statement admitting that the work is based on actual people or events, this may be sufficient to make the work libelous. The acknowledgment, preface, afterword, or other statement may be admissible in a lawsuit.

10.8   Perform a Careful Prepublication Review

Once your manuscript is completed, you need to review it carefully prior to publication to make sure that it will not libel anyone. By taking the following steps, in most cases you will be able to identify conspicuously libelous passages in time to make necessary changes prior to publication.

10.8.1   List All People, Organizations, and Products

First, carefully review the manuscript line by line and page by page, and make a list of every person, company, product, and organization identified, mentioned, or described in any way. Also be wary of broad generalizations that might apply to more than one person if they can describe a group of 25 or fewer people. Make sure you review any preface, acknowledgment, or afterword along with the primary text.

10.8.2   Check Headlines and Captions

Watch out for headlines and photo captions, too. Headlines can be defamatory by themselves or can imply false innuendo about a story or a photograph. For example, a headline stating, "Man Convicted of Robbery" accompanying a news story about a man who was simply arrested for robbery but not *convicted* may be defamatory. Make sure that headlines accurately and fairly indicate the content of the material they accompany. Similarly, make sure the names in photo captions are spelled correctly and correspond to the right people.

10.8.3   List People Not Mentioned Who Could Also Be Affected

As you review the manuscript, also make a list of any person, company, product, or organization that although not specifically identified or mentioned could be affected or identified. This includes people and organizations that are identified by implication and that are identified with a product or place.

10.8.4   List All Fictional Characters and Events

Be on the lookout for unintentional defamation. Make a list of all fictional names, businesses, companies, and characters that appear in the work, together with the name of the town or city in which they live, reside, or maintain offices in the work. Use telephone books, business catalogs, and other reference materials to verify that no actual people, characters, businesses, or companies exist in those places with the same names as those contained in your work. If they do, you should change the name of the person, character, company, or business in your work and repeat the process, to make sure that the new name does not coincide with an actual person or entity. Very often, libel and privacy lawsuits arise because an author created a fictitious character who, coincidentally, had the same name and lived in the same place as a real person, prompting the real person to sue. Remember, an author's actual intent is irrelevant. The key question is whether an ordinary reader would believe that an imaginary character named X as actually a real person named X.

10.8.5   Pay Attention to the Tone

It's also important to be wary of the tone of the manuscript. Although the tone itself probably cannot defame anyone, a jury might find a malicious or negative tone to be evidence of bad faith or ill will against the person described. Therefore, pay extra-close attention to statements made in a negative or accusatory tone. You may want to change the tone to make it more friendly or double-check the accuracy of the allegations made when the tone is negative.

> **Tip**
> ☞ Be especially careful with books that are at high risk for libel claims. These include probing investigative efforts; biographies; books supported by confidential sources; works attacking individuals, businesses, or defined groups; works patterned after or based on true events; and works with controversial content.

10.8.6   Connect All Accusations with People Described

After you have made a list of all people described in your manuscript, whether directly or by implication, you need to make a list of the allegations stated about each person, entity, organization, or product. If any accusation or description could reasonably imply some other accusation or facts, make a list of these implied facts as well. You now have a list of all the people who are likely to sue you for libel, together with a list of each allegation made or implied about them. While it is absolutely necessary to list all of the negative or embarrassing statements made about each person, organization, and product, it is also helpful to list the positive and nonembarrassing statements made about them as well.

10.8.7   Determine Whether Any of the Statements Is Libelous

Now that you have a list of all statements made about all of the people, products, and entities described in your manuscript, you are able to evaluate whether any of the statements is potentially libelous. Remember, a libelous statement is a false statement of fact that is embarrassing or that causes damage to a living person's (or existing business's) reputation. For purposes of your prepublication review, any negative, embarrassing, or unflattering statement should be considered potentially libelous. Thus, pay attention to those types of statements to make sure you can adequately defend a lawsuit if one is brought.

10.8.8   Determine Whether You Can Defend a Claim

If you spot any potentially defamatory statements, it is now time to determine whether you have a good defense against a libel action. Make sure that you can present a valid defense for each of the negative, embarrassing, or unflattering statements made about the people described in your manuscript.

Otherwise, it is generally advisable to alter the potentially defamatory passage (e.g., change it from a pejorative statement of fact to a protected statement of opinion), or remove it altogether.

To help you evaluate whether you have a defense, it is useful to do the following:

1. *Itemize all evidence that supports the statement.*   For each potentially defamatory accusation and statement, itemize all information and evidence available to you that supports your claim and on which you could rely to prove that the statement or accusation is true.

2. *Ask yourself whether you would be upset.*   It's often helpful to ask yourself, "If the story or accusation were about me, would I believe that the writer used good faith and took reasonable steps to verify the accuracy of the statement and to publish the truth based on the information available?" If the answer is no, it's time to start thinking about removing the statement, changing the objectionable passage, obtaining a release, doing additional research to attempt to verify the accuracy of the statement, or seeing an attorney to determine the chances of winning a libel suit.

3. *Determine whether a valid defense or privilege applies.*   You must determine whether you would be able to successfully defend a lawsuit for each accusation made in your manuscript. This means that you must determine whether you will be able to prove a valid defense (truth, opinion, rhetorical hyperbole, or consent) or whether a valid privilege applies. List all of the facts, evidence, and information available to you to help prove any defense or privilege.

10.8.9   If You Can't Avoid a Potential Claim, Seek Legal Advice

Sometimes, the best way to avoid lawsuits is by getting advice from a competent attorney. Prepublication review by a libel lawyer can be an extremely important part of the publishing process, especially with high-risk works. Unfortunately, a libel review by a competent attorney can be costly, but the cost of defending a libel action is guaranteed to be much higher. Find out whether your publishing company will have an attorney review the manuscript, and, if not, find an attorney to review or *vet* (evaluate) the manuscript for you before you deliver it to the publisher. Because the cost of reviewing all manuscripts is prohibitive, most publishers will have their attorneys review only those manuscripts that they believe pose a significant risk of a lawsuit. For that matter, even if the publishing company will have its legal department review the manuscript for you, it is a good practice to have your own attorney review a high-risk manuscript before you submit it to the publishing company. Why should you go to this trouble and expense? Because you are ultimately responsible for the costs of defending a lawsuit and will have a contractual obligation to indemnify the publisher for expenses if a lawsuit is brought.

10.9   Obtain Libel Insurance

In addition to doing a careful prepublication review, you can minimize your liability for libel claims by having your publisher name you as an "additional insured" party on the publisher's media-liability insurance policy. If you are a self-publisher or your publisher will not name you as an additional insured on the publisher's insurance policy, you may be able to obtain your own media-risk insurance policy. A publisher's liability insurance policy, or "media-risk" policy, can provide insurance for the costs incurred in defending a defamation lawsuit, as well as for any judgment. Media liability insurance is discussed in greater detail in Chapter 13.

10.10   What If Someone Threatens to Sue You?

If despite your efforts someone threatens to sue you, take the threat seriously. However, do not admit guilt. Politely advise the party that you will have your attorney review the matter, and do so immediately. In no event should you agree to publish a retraction without first consulting with your attorney. However, you must act quickly. Under many state statutes you have only a limited amount of time in which to publish a withdrawal.

Basics of Publicity and Privacy

The *right of publicity* is the right of a person to control the commercial use of his or her name, likeness, or identity. The *right of privacy*, a related right, protects people from the publication of private, intimate, and embarrassing information pertaining to them. It does so, mainly, by punishing authors and publishers who publish true but embarrassing facts about a person.

The law of privacy, which varies from state to state, can be broken down into at least three subcategories: (1) the publication of intimate and embarrassing facts about a person; (2) the publication of facts that create a "false light," or impression, about a person that is highly offensive; and (3) the intentional intrusion upon someone's privacy.

Unlike defamation claims, publicity and privacy claims usually arise from the publication of truthful information. Therefore, authors and publishers need to familiarize themselves with the basics of publicity and privacy laws to avoid lawsuits and claims. Bear in mind that right of publicity and privacy claims can usually be avoided by obtaining written releases.

11.1   The Right of Publicity

The right of publicity gives every individual the right to control and profit from the commercial use of his or her name or likeness. Like copyrights and trademarks, the right of publicity is a valuable property right. Unlike the right of privacy, which protects against mental anguish for publication of embarrassing or intimate facts, the right of publicity gives people a property right in certain features of their identity. The right of publicity protects against the loss of financial gain by giving a person the right to prevent the unauthorized use of his or her name for commercial purposes. Without a right of publicity, actors, recording artists, and sports figures wouldn't get paid for endorsements and advertisements featuring their name, voice, signature, photograph, or likeness. Thus, a person who knowingly uses another's name or likeness on or in connection with products, merchandise, goods, or services without the person's consent is liable for violating that person's right of publicity.

11.1.1 First Amendment Protection

The law strikes a balance between free speech rights and the right of publicity. To accommodate the First Amendment, there are two general exceptions to the rule that you can't use a person's name or likeness for commercial purposes without his or her consent: (1) the "newsworthiness" exception, and (2) the "incidental use" exception.

1. *The "newsworthiness" exception.* Under this exception, a person cannot object to the use of his or her likeness in a publication dealing with a matter of general public interest, unless there is no real relationship between the person and the subject matter of the publication, or the use is false or misleading. This rule applies to both "hard" news and matters of legitimate interest or concern, including sports and entertainment. Therefore, generally, a well-known person cannot stop the use of his or her name or likeness in connection with an unauthorized biography. The protection of the right of free expression is so important that even where a right of publicity is recognized, the public's right to know what prominent people have done, or what has happened to them, is generally indulged.

    However, there are limitations. The use must be neither explicitly misleading nor a thinly veiled commercial advertisement for a product or service. Thus, with an unauthorized biography, you should include an appropriate disclaimer stating that the book was not prepared, approved, or licensed by the subject of the work. While a disclaimer won't prevent someone from suing you, it might discourage a claim that the work misleads consumers into believing it was authorized. For sample disclaimers, see Appendix D.

2. *The "incidental use" exception.* Generally, it does not violate a person's right of publicity if you merely mention the person's name, or depict his or her likeness, incidental to a privileged use. For example, one court has held that the unauthorized use on a book jacket of a quotation from a book review comparing a new book to the work of a well-known person was a permissible incidental use. Comparing

one author to another is of interest to the public, who must decide whether to purchase a particular author's book. Similarly, using a photograph of a celebrity on the cover of an unauthorized biography that is later used to advertise that book is permissible.

11.1.2 The Right of Publicity Varies from State to State

There is no federal right of publicity—or privacy—law. The right of publicity is governed by state law. In some states, such as California, specific statutes limit the types of uses that constitute a commercial use. In other states, common law—as distinguished from the laws passed by state legislatures—governs the right of publicity.

11.1.3 What Constitutes a "Name or Likeness"?

The law doesn't require a person's full, formal name to be used before the person's right of publicity is infringed on. In fact, even a caricature or sketch of a person, or the use of the person's nickname, may be sufficient to violate someone's right of publicity. Even if a person's actual photograph or name is not used, if the person is identifiable from the context, that may constitute use of that person's identity as far as the law is concerned.

Indeed, courts have held the use of a person's first name, a person's abandoned birth name, a surname alone, the slogan "Here's Johnny" (to identify Johnny Carson), a photograph of a woman's backside without showing her face, a Vanna White-like robot, and even distinctive markings on a race car and a customized motorcycle sufficient to support a lawsuit. In fact, a person's right of publicity can be infringed on even when a fictitious name is used, if the plaintiff is reasonably identifiable from the other facts presented.

11.1.4 To Whom Does the Right of Publicity Apply?

The protections accorded by the right of publicity are governed by state law. In some states, the right of publicity applies only to people who are celebrities. In other states, any person has the right to sue if the person's name or likeness is used for a commercial purpose. Because most books and magazines are distributed widely throughout the United States, authors and publishers should be ready to defend a lawsuit in any state. Therefore, authors and publishers must assume that the right is not limited to celebrities and that anyone can sue if his or her name or likeness is used for a commercial purpose.

Dead celebrities (or their heirs) have rights, too. Because the right of publicity is a property right, it can be licensed and sold. In some states, the right of publicity can be exercised, or licensed, by a dead celebrity's heirs. For example, Elvis Presley may be dead, but his estate actively enforces Elvis's right of publicity.

11.1.5   What Constitutes a Commercial Use?

Generally, a *commercial use* encompasses the use of a person's name or likeness in an advertisement or in connection with the sale of a product or service. For example, the use of a celebrity's photograph on a poster that is sold in stores is almost always deemed to be commercial in nature. Just because a publisher operates for profit, however, does not—for First Amendment purposes—make a book a commercial use. However, the use of a person's photograph in an advertisement for a related book or magazine article concerning that individual will usually be considered editorial in nature and necessary to accurately describe the contents of the book or magazine. Thus, Elizabeth Taylor would not prevail if she attempted to enjoin a publisher from using her name or image in connection with an unauthorized biography entitled *The Elizabeth Taylor Story*.

11.1.6   What about Advertisements for a Book?

In most cases, publishers can use a person's name or likeness to promote and advertise a book. However, the use of that person's name or likeness must be reasonably related to the contents of the book and constitutes an accurate representation of the contents of the book. For example, President Clinton's name and photograph can be used in advertisements for an unauthorized biography of President Clinton because the photograph is reasonably related to the contents of the book and is indicative of its subject matter. However, the unauthorized use of Clint Eastwood's photograph or name to promote a book about someone else may constitute an invasion of Mr. Eastwood's right of publicity, assuming that Mr. Eastwood has no reasonable connection to that book.

> **TIP** The use of a person's name or likeness in a book's title or on a book's cover is usually considered an editorial and not a commercial use if the name or likeness is reasonably related to the subject matter of the book, and the use is neither false nor misleading.

11.1.7   What about Editorial Uses?

Due to First Amendment considerations, the use of a person's name or likeness for scholarship, cultural, historical, educational, political, and public interest purposes or for news reporting does not invade a person's right of publicity. Therefore, as a general rule, the use of a person's photograph in connection with a related book or news article is permissible, even if the work is more entertaining than newsworthy.

This applies both to hard news and to articles involving matters of legitimate public interest or concern. Be careful, though, as many courts hold that if you have an actual intention to injure the plaintiff, even if the content is newsworthy, or of legitimate public interest, your bad-faith intention may outweigh the newsworthiness of the article and may give rise to a lawsuit. This often applies to tabloidlike articles that purport to be true, but are, in fact, fabrications. For example, it would be a violation of a celebrity's rights to falsely claim she bore a child out of wedlock, merely to sell more books or magazines.

11.1.8   What about Fictionalized Accounts Based on Real People?

Like the newsworthiness exception, when someone's name or likeness is used in a fictional account, provided the use is artistically relevant to the story and clearly presented as fiction, it *may* find protection under the First Amendment.

In one noteworthy case, a federal court held that a novel containing a fictional account of an event in the life of author Agatha Christie did not constitute an invasion of the right of publicity because the novel was clearly labeled as fiction, and it was an artistic and editorial use, as opposed to a commercial one. However, a factual misrepresentation in a work of fiction that is embarrassing could cause liability for defamation or false light invasion of privacy.

> **TIP** ☞ Even in cases involving editorial or artistic uses, the use of a person's name, photograph, or likeness must still be reasonably related to some informational or cultural purpose of legitimate public concern, and not merely intended to exploit the subject's identity for pecuniary gain.

11.1.9   Who Can Sue?

In the majority of states, the law allows only a living person to sue for a violation of the right of publicity. However, in a handful of states—including California, Florida, Kentucky, Nebraska, Nevada, New Jersey, Oklahoma, Tennessee, and Virginia—the right of publicity survives a person's death, and the heirs of a deceased celebrity are permitted to sue for invasion of the right of publicity. In some states, the right of publicity must be exploited during a person's lifetime in order to survive that person's death.

11.1.10   What Other Rights Can Be Infringed?

It is important to note that the same circumstances that give rise to an action for infringement of the right of publicity can also give rise to a lawsuit on other grounds. For example, the unauthorized use of a person's name or likeness for a commercial purpose may also give rise to a lawsuit for unfair competition under federal and state unfair competition law.

11.2   The Right of Privacy: Publication of Private and Embarrassing Facts

It is an invasion of privacy to publish or to publicize private and intimate facts about a person. The law prevents the publication of private information when the information is of a nature that would be highly offensive to a reasonable person and the information is not of any legitimate concern to the public. Bear in mind that everything that might be of interest to the public is not necessarily of "legitimate" concern to the public if it doesn't relate to a topic of public interest.

11.2.1   Truth Is No Defense

While truth is always a defense to a claim of libel, it is not a defense to a claim of invasion of privacy. Indeed, because the law of privacy protects against the publication of private and embarrassing information, the fact that the information is true makes it even more embarrassing. Therefore, the truth is no defense to a claim of invasion of privacy by publication of private embarrassing facts.

11.2.2   Public Records May Be Published

To sustain a lawsuit for disclosure of private and embarrassing facts, published material must be of a highly personal nature. Therefore, authors and publishers are generally free to publish information that is generally known or available, such as names and addresses and information contained in public records, such as birth, marriage, and military records. Similarly, once a government agency has disclosed information or made it publicly available, it is generally considered to be public information and will not give rise to an action for invasion of the right of privacy.

11.2.3   Newsworthy Information May Be Published

If published information is newsworthy or of legitimate concern to the public, its publication will not be actionable. This includes the publication of information pertaining to legal proceedings, arrests, suicides, accidents, fires, and similar reports. In one notable case, the Supreme Court held that the publication of the name of a rape victim did not constitute a publication of private embarrassing facts because the information was obtained from official court records, which were open to public inspection. Discretion should be exercised when disclosing intimate and embarrassing facts relating to private individuals, since the public interest benefit of such disclosures may be more difficult to justify.

11.2.4   Various Types of Private Materials Are Protected

The types of materials and information that are usually protected by the right of privacy include private letters, information pertaining to sexual orientation or sexual relations, information about a person's wealth or health, and other information pertaining to a person's private affairs. Likewise, if information is sensationalized or published in a manner that would outrage an average person, courts generally hold the publication to be sufficiently offensive to constitute an invasion of privacy. For example, publication of nude or seminude photographs of subjects without their consent may be sufficiently offensive to constitute an invasion of privacy. Publication of an individual's medical records or psychiatric history may also be actionable.

11.2.5 It Makes a Difference Who the Plaintiff Is

As with defamation cases, courts distinguish between private and public plaintiffs in cases involving the publication of private embarrassing facts. If the plaintiff is a public official or a public figure and the information relates to some newsworthy or publicly important aspect of the person's life, the publication will not constitute an offense. Generally, a public official for purposes of defamation law is treated as a public person for purposes of privacy law. Similarly, a public figure for purposes of defamation law is also a public figure for purposes of privacy law.

11.3 The Right of Privacy: False Light Invasion of Privacy

The second type of invasion of privacy claim arises from publications that place an individual in a false light or create a false impression that a reasonable person would find highly offensive. This area of privacy law is very similar to defamation insofar as it seeks to prohibit false impressions about a person that an ordinary person would consider highly offensive. In fact, not all states recognize false light as a separate cause of action, distinct from defamation.

11.3.1 How Does False Light Differ from Libel Law?

Unlike libel law, in order for a publication to constitute false light, the statement must be highly offensive to an ordinary person. False light also differs from libel law in that there need not be any injury to reputation. The law of false light invasion of privacy is designed to provide damages for hurt feelings and embarrassment, as opposed to loss of reputation.

11.3.2 What Are the Elements of a False Light Claim?

The technical requirements for a claim of false light are threefold: (1) the impression created must be highly offensive to a reasonable person, (2) the defendant (author, publisher, or both) must have published with the requisite degree of fault, and (3) the plaintiff must be an identifiable living person.

TIP   Caption your photographs carefully and accurately. A misleading caption that creates a false impression about an individual could give rise to a false light lawsuit.

11.3.3   What Types of Publications Constitute False Light?

Very often, in false light cases, the false impression comes from innuendo or the contextual use of misleading photographs or information. Therefore, false impressions that do not rise to the level of defamation may still give rise to an action for false light privacy. Typically, false light claims arise in four circumstances: (1) when facts are distorted or omitted to create a false impression of what actually happened; (2) when facts are mixed with fiction or are embellished with fictional, exaggerated, or imaginative details or dialogue; (3) when actual events are fictionalized or dramatized; and (4) when photographs are printed in conjunction with unrelated headlines or captions or unrelated stories.

CASE AND COMMENT

Regarding the case of *Parnell v. Booth Newspapers, Inc.*, 572 F. Supp. 909 (W.D. Mich. 1983), in 1981, a local Michigan newspaper published an article about prostitution in the vicinity of a business district. The newspaper sent a photographer to the area one evening to take pictures to accompany the story. The photographer saw a woman come out of a bar and attempt to carry on conversations with passersby and then observed the same woman having a brief conversation with someone in a car. The photographer speculated that the woman was a prostitute and took a photograph of her. The photograph ended up in the newspaper accompanying the story on prostitution, and the woman in the photograph sued the newspaper for defamation, false light invasion of privacy, and infliction of emotional distress, claiming that she was falsely imputed to be a prostitute. The appeals court held that the plaintiff had made a sufficient case to proceed to a jury trial.

Even if a photograph is reasonably related to an accompanying article, if it is misleading and would be highly offensive to a reasonable person, it could lead to a false light claim.

11.4   Intrusion on One's Solitude

Finally, the right of privacy really does include the right to be left alone. If you intrude on a person's solitude or seclusion in an offensive manner, you have also invaded that individual's privacy.

11.4.1   What Constitutes Intrusion?

When you interfere with people's right to be left alone in circumstances where they would expect some privacy, you have invaded their right of privacy. Traditionally, intrusion claims arise when an author or reporter engages in hidden surveillance or commits a physical trespass (such as breaking into someone's home, opening someone's mail, or going through someone's garbage). Publication is *not* required.

> **CAUTION**   Watch out for photographs taken by hidden cameras and statements recorded by hidden microphones or hidden tape recorders. They could lead to claims of invasion of privacy, as well as criminal liability under state and federal wiretapping laws.

While merely obtaining an interview under false pretenses normally does not constitute an intrusion on solitude, using a hidden microphone or a hidden camera to surreptitiously record or photograph a conversation or meeting may constitute an invasion of privacy.

It is important to note that the intrusion need not include breaking and entering or actual physical intrusion in order to be actionable. It need only be offensive. In a notorious case involving Jacqueline Kennedy Onassis and photographer Ron Galella, a federal court found that Mr. Galella's pattern of following Mrs. Onassis and her children was unreasonable and violated her right to privacy. In that case, the court ordered Mr. Galella to remain at a distance of at least 25 feet from Mrs. Onassis at all times.

11.4.2   What Laws Pertain to the Recording of Telephone Conversations?

Whether a party to a telephone conversation can record the conversation is a matter of state law. Many states require that all parties to a conversation must consent to any recording of the conversation. Other states require only one of the parties to consent. If you do not know the law of your state (and the state in which the other party to the telephone conversation resides), you should obtain the consent of all of the parties to the telephone conversation before recording it, to avoid liability for invasion of privacy, as well as criminal liability under wiretapping laws. The use of a telephone tap will always give rise to a claim for invasion of privacy, as well as criminal liability for violation of state and federal laws against wiretapping.

11.4.3   What about Undercover Investigations?

In some states, an unreasonably intrusive investigation may give rise to an action for invasion of privacy. For example, in California, a private investigator's deceptive entry into the hospital room of an accident victim was deemed to constitute an unreasonably intrusive investigation. Similar activity, such as a probe into someone's medical records or through someone's garbage, can also constitute an invasion of privacy.

In one notable case, reporters pretended to seek medical advice from a doctor and used hidden cameras and tape recorders to record their conversations with the doctor in his home. The reporters set out to prove that the doctor was really just a journeyman plumber who was practicing medicine without a license by healing people with herbs and minerals. The reporters went to the doctor's house and told him that a friend had referred them for treatment. The information the reporters obtained, together with a photograph taken with a hidden camera during the visit, was later published in *Life Magazine* to portray the doctor as a "quack." The court held that the reporters had invaded the doctor's privacy by intruding on his solitude in that case.

11.4.4   What If I Stay on Public Property?

Trespassing on private property to obtain information usually constitutes an invasion of privacy. However, as a general rule, writers and photographers may remain on public property or property open to the public to obtain information. Likewise, they may report on or take a picture of something on private property that is readily viewable from a public space. However, in these circumstances, the subject photographed or reported on must be readily viewable from a public place with the naked eye. Taking a picture, from a public spot, of a person a mile away, using a powerful telephoto lens, may constitute an unreasonable intrusion under some circumstances.

11.4.5   Is Publication Required?

Unlike libel law, in which publication is necessary, to constitute intrusion, publication is not necessary to make out a claim. It is the manner of news or information gathering that constitutes the violation of the right of privacy, not the publication of the information. Even if you decide *not* to publish the information or photograph obtained by intrusive means, you can still be sued for invasion of privacy.

11.5   Who Can Sue for Invasion of Privacy?

Ordinarily, only a living person can sue for invasion of privacy. While dead people cannot have their privacy invaded and cannot have their feelings hurt, if people's rights are infringed while they are alive, in most cases their estate will have the right to bring a lawsuit on their behalf. One exception to the general rule exists with respect to the right of publicity. As described previously, in several states, the right of publicity continues after death, in which case the estate of a deceased person can bring an action for invasion of the right of publicity.

11.6   What Are the Defenses to Invasion of Privacy?

Because the nature of the three privacy rights differs, the defenses to these claims also vary. While consent is always a defense to any claim of invasion of privacy, the other defenses diverge.

11.6.1   Consent and Release

Consent is always an absolute defense to invasion of privacy. Thus, once a subject has signed a properly drafted release or a consent form, he or she has given his or her consent to the publication and has waived or relinquished the right to sue for invasion of privacy. As with libel law, where feasible, the consent in a formal release should be in writing, or on tape. While an oral consent may also be enforceable under the laws of some states, it is always difficult to prove, and an oral consent is sometimes revocable under state law. Therefore, as always, you should get the consent or release in writing.

It is important to remember that the consent given by the subject may be limited to a particular publication or particular information. Therefore, when consent is given, the publisher and author cannot exceed the scope of the consent; if they do, they may be subject to liability for invasion of privacy.

11.6.2   Death

Once a person has died, his or her privacy cannot be invaded. After all, a dead person cannot be embarrassed by a publication. There are, however, two important caveats relating to this defense. First, as discussed previously, the right to prevent misappropriation of one's likeness for commercial purposes survives the death of a person in many states. Second, death is a defense only for publications occurring after the plaintiff's death. If an article is published about a person while the person is alive and the person dies soon after the publication, the plaintiff's heirs usually have the right to bring or to continue prosecuting a lawsuit on the deceased person's behalf.

11.6.3   Public Information

A defense to a claim of publication of private, embarrassing facts is the proof that the information or facts disclosed were public information. This includes both information that has already been disclosed to the public and information that is newsworthy or of legitimate concern to the public. Remember, the law prohibits the disclosure of private and intimate facts only.

11.6.4   Inoffensiveness

When dealing with claims of publication of private, embarrassing facts and claims of false light, the disclosure or portrayal must be both embarrassing and highly offensive in nature. If the facts disclosed would not be highly offensive to a reasonable person, they will not give rise to a lawsuit.

11.6.5   Truth

Unlike libel law, where truth is an absolute defense, in privacy law, the truth is generally not a defense. That is because it is not the falsity but, rather, the way in which the information was obtained or is used that makes it embarrassing.

11.6.6   Newsworthiness

Another defense to claims of disclosure of private, embarrassing facts is newsworthiness, or information of legitimate public interest. However, keep in mind that the newsworthiness defense may weaken over time. As time elapses, information that was once of legitimate public concern can become private. Thus, be careful when publishing old embarrassing or highly offensive facts.

CHECKLIST: **Publicity and Privacy**

Right of Publicity
- ☐ Is the name, photograph, or other identifying feature of an actual person used?
- ☐ Is a celebrity's name or persona implied from the context, although the person's name is not specifically mentioned?
- ☐ Is the name, likeness, photograph, or description used to sell a product or service?
- ☐ Will the publisher derive a commercial or direct economic benefit from the use of the name or photograph? If so, is the name or likeness used to convey newsworthy information?
- ☐ Is the name or likeness used to provide an example of the editorial content of the work?
- ☐ Have you obtained a written release or license?

Private and Embarrassing Facts
- ☐ Are the facts embarrassing or of an intimate nature?
- ☐ Would the average person be outraged by the publication or think that the publication exceeded the bounds of decency? If so, is the information newsworthy or of legitimate concern to the public?
- ☐ Are the facts available from public records, or have they previously been published?
- ☐ Are the facts about a private individual, as opposed to a public official or celebrity?
- ☐ Is the subject living?
- ☐ Have you obtained a written release or consent from the subject?

False Light
- ☐ Are any facts distorted or omitted to suggest or imply certain conclusions or other facts?

☐ Are any facts or circumstances exaggerated, fictionalized, or embellished? If so, would a reasonable reader get a false impression
of the truth or of the subject?

☐ If a photograph is used, is it reasonably related to the story, headline, and caption that accompany it?

☐ Would the story, the photograph, or the intimations be offensive to a
reasonable reader? If so, is the subject living?

☐ Is the subject a public figure or a private individual?

☐ Is the gist or the sting of the implication true or substantially true?

☐ Can you prove that it is true?

☐ Have you obtained a written release?

Intrusion

☐ Was the information obtained through theft or other illegal conduct?

☐ Would a reasonable person find either the published material or the
way it was obtained highly offensive in manner?

☐ Did you obtain the information by conducting an unauthorized investigation through personal items or personal records?

☐ If any of the preceding are true, was the information also available
from public records?

☐ Would you consider your actions to be offensive or to exceed the
bounds of decency?

☐ If the information isn't publicly known or newsworthy, have you obtained consent or a written release from the subject?

☐ If photographs are to be published, were they taken when the subject was in a nonpublic place and might have expected privacy? If
so, were the photographs taken from a public place, and was the
subject readily viewable with the naked eye?

☐ Is the subject matter highly personal in nature?

When and How to Obtain a Release

Courts place a great weight on an individual's consent to be interviewed, or to have his or her image reproduced in a book or article. For example, consent is a complete defense to invasion of privacy. A release can also protect against a libel suit. While consent can be implied by someone's conduct—or even be given orally—it is always best to obtain a formal, signed consent. Consent forms, or "releases," are simply the best way to avoid a lawsuit.

Of course, it is not always possible (or necessary) to obtain a written release. As we discuss in Chapter 9, if you are writing about a newsworthy event or public figure, provided your report is fair and accurate, a release is not legally required. Similarly, candid photographs taken in a public place to illustrate an article of general public interest, provided the photographs are not embarrassing or do not place someone in an unflattering light, generally do not require a release.

12.1 When Do I Need to Obtain an Interview Release?

While your publishing agreement may only require you to obtain permission to use copyrighted works, if your work is controversial, you may want to obtain written releases stating that the person you've interviewed has given you his or her consent. If feasible, releases should be signed during the interview session. This way, if an interviewee refuses to sign, you can remove the passage, or, alternatively, proceed with caution—alert for potential libel, publicity, and privacy issues. While a formal written release is preferable, oral consent recorded on tape, or before witnesses, may be equally valid. Unfortunately, oral releases are always less comprehensive than written releases, and are often ambiguous, too. It is important to note that if you go beyond the scope of an interviewee's consent, you lose your consent defense.

12.2   What If the Subject Tells Me Something "Off the Record"?

If you promise interviewees to keep the information they give you confidential, the law will hold you to your promise. Therefore, if a person consents to an interview, subject to your agreement not to disclose certain information, or the person asks to confide certain information to you on a "not for publication" or "off the record" basis, your promise not to publish or disclose that information will be enforceable. Absent a subject's express written consent, the use of any material given to you under a promise of confidentiality or with a condition that it is off the record can give rise to a lawsuit.

12.3   What If a Source Asks for Anonymity?

Promises that a source will not be identified or will not be identifiable are enforceable. Where anonymity has been promised, both the author and the publisher have a duty to disguise the source's identity sufficiently so that the source will not be identifiable. Even if the source's name is not disclosed, if the identity of the person is reasonably recognizable, the author and the publisher may be liable for damages.

CASE AND COMMENT

In *Ruzicka v. Conde Nast Publications, Inc.*, 999 F. 2d 1319 (8th Cir. 1993), a writer for *Glamour* magazine promised anonymity to a Minnesota lawyer who agreed to relate a story about therapist-patient sexual abuse. The lawyer related the story, based on the understanding that her identity would not be revealed. Even though the writer changed the lawyer's name in the story, the lawyer was still identified as a "Minneapolis attorney" who had served on a state task force that helped to write the Minnesota law criminalizing therapist-patient sex. A lawsuit arose, and the court held that the writer had broken her promise to hide Ms. Ruzicka's identity.

Merely changing a person's name is not sufficient to hide the person's identity if other facts are disclosed from which the identity of the person is reasonably identifiable. A writer must disguise the source's identity sufficiently so that the source will not be identifiable.

12.4   What If a Person Gives Me Confidential Business Information?

Business information is protected by law if it is considered a "trade secret." A *trade secret* is confidential business information not known to the public, such as a business's list of customers or a proprietary chemical formula. Trade secrets are generally protected under state law, and the laws vary from state to state. However, most state trade secret laws protect confidential customer lists, supplier lists, manufacturing processes, and other confidential business materials that a company seeks to keep private and confidential because its disclosure would have significant negative consequences for the company's business.

> **TIP**   Be wary of disgruntled employees who want to provide you with confidential business information to publish. The information could constitute a trade secret, and you may be liable for damages to the company for publishing it.

12.5   What Types of Releases Do I Need for the Use of a Photograph?

Because a photograph is protected by copyright, permission is usually required from the copyright owner of the photographic image. In addition, a separate release may be necessary from any recognizable individuals depicted in the photograph if the photograph is used in a commercial context or in a manner that could give rise to a claim of false light (see Section 11.3). A release in this context will protect the photographer from invasion of privacy and commercial misappropriation lawsuits.

12.5.1   What about Releases from Photographic Models?

When the photograph contains any models who have agreed to have their photograph taken (whether or not they are professional models), contractual issues—as well as libel, privacy, and publicity issues—may arise. When models consent to having their photographs taken, they do not necessarily consent to *all* uses of those photographs. Therefore, it is advisable to obtain a release to avoid any later disputes or lawsuits. If you are relying on a release obtained by a third party—a freelance photographer, for example—ask to see the release to ensure that it covers the intended uses. You should also have the photographer warrant that he or she has the right to license you rights. In addition, the photographer should indemnify you from any legal actions if the release is flawed.

| **TIP** | Beware of photographs depicting professional models. Professional models often have agreements with photographers that limit the uses of the photograph, require approval over the photograph's use, or require additional compensation if the photograph is published. |

12.5.2   What about a Photograph of a Celebrity?

While the photograph of a celebrity may generally be published for newsworthy or public interest purposes, when the photograph is used to sell or advertise products, goods, or services, right of publicity issues arise. In these cases, a release from the subject of the photograph must be obtained.

12.5.3   What about Photographs of Minors?

Beware of photographs depicting children and young adults under 21 years of age. As a general rule, a parent or guardian must sign the release on behalf of a minor. While in most states people over the age of 18 can sign contracts, in a few states the age is 19 or even 21. Check the law of your state on what age constitutes a minor. Also, be aware that many states allow minors to withdraw consent when they become adults, although this is less likely to be tolerated with paid professional models.

12.5.4   What about News and Political Photographs?

As a general rule, under the First Amendment, photographs may be freely published (with the permission of the photographer, that is) in connection with news, political, social, and economic events. Keep in mind that entertainment news, as well as hard news, is protected under the First Amendment. Remember, once again, that photographs with recognizable people should never be used for a commercial purpose without the consent of the subjects.

12.5.5 What about Street Scenes?

Releases are generally not required from people who are identifiable in a photograph of a street or a public place, provided that the photograph is reasonably related to the subject matter and the identifiable people are not the focus of the photograph. However, if the photograph is used in a derogatory or offensive manner or in a manner that is unrelated to the surrounding editorial context, the individuals who are identified could have some grounds to sue for false light or defamation. In that case, a release may be necessary. As an example of a permitted use, a photograph of the famous Rockefeller Center Ice Rink in New York City may be used to illustrate a book about Rockefeller Center or about New York tourist attractions, although many people may be identifiable.

12.5.6 What about Identifiable Buildings?

Unique building designs are sometimes used as a trademark or service mark. For example, the famous TransAmerica Insurance building is used as a trademark by TransAmerica. If the use of the photograph might imply some type of sponsorship or approval of a product or service, you should get a release from the owner of the building. When getting a release, make sure that you obtain the signature of the owner of the building or, if the building is owned by a corporation or business entity, the signature of an authorized agent, officer, or director. The building manager also usually has the required authority to grant permissions (see Appendix C, Form F, "Property Release").

12.5.7 What about Photographs Portraying Sex or Nudity?

Always beware of photographs containing sex or nudity. These often give rise to invasion of privacy lawsuits. Whenever a photograph portrays sex (whether simulated or actual) or nudity (whether full or partial), a release is required. The release should specify that the photograph contains nudity or sex and must clearly acknowledge that the subject consents to the exploitation of the photograph. Otherwise, the author and the publisher will be open to claims of invasion of privacy. In one case, a New York court found that a magazine publisher had defamed a male model by including his photograph in a sexually suggestive magazine without his consent.

While a nude photograph of a person who is under the age of 18 is not necessarily "child pornography," the federal child-pornography laws and most state child-pornography laws are interpreted very broadly and can encompass a nude photograph of a minor, even if the photograph does not contain sex or simulated sex. Photographs depicting minors engaged in sex or even simulated sex may violate both federal and state laws and can lead to severe criminal penalties for authors and publishers, including criminal fines, destruction of all copies of the work, and even imprisonment.

Always make sure that the models are at least 18 years old. Whenever a photograph contains sexually explicit content, such as sex acts or even simulated sex acts, federal law requires that the photographer and the publisher obtain and keep on file photocopies of at least one form of identification (e.g., a driver's license) for each model or subject proving that the subject is more than 18 years old. This federal law applies to books, magazines, and other printed materials, as well as to films and videotapes that are made after November 1, 1990. Under the laws of some states (which can be even more onerous than federal law), the signature of a parent or guardian may be necessary if the model is under the age of 21.

TIP Federal law requires publishers to keep on file a copy of a driver's license or other form of identification for all models when sex or simulated sex is involved. This ensures that all models are at least 18 years old. The law further requires all publishers and book distributors to provide a notice on the published work stating where the records are kept.

12.5.8   Do Stock Photographs and Images Require Releases?

Just because a photograph or illustration is in a stock house's collection, or it purports to be royalty free, that does not necessarily mean that the photographer has obtained required releases from models. Always ask the stock house whether the underlying rights have been cleared, and obtain some type of verification that appropriate releases have been obtained from all models. If you aren't sure, and you think that the manner in which you intend to use the stock photograph may lead to a libel or invasion of privacy or publicity claim, you may want to use another photograph or try to obtain a release from the subject, assuming that you can track down the subject. Never use a stock photograph as a commercial endorsement or in connection with the advertisement or sale of a product unless you are positive that a model release has been obtained and permission for such use has been specifically granted by the subject.

Media Perils Insurance

Most author-publisher agreements require authors to indemnify and hold their publisher harmless for the costs of any claims arising from the content of the book or from the author's failure to obtain required permissions. Insurance policies are available to publishers and authors to protect against media perils and to cover the costs of any claims. These policies generally cover claims of copyright infringement, trademark infringement, defamation, and invasion of privacy. Some policies even cover claims of misappropriation of ideas or infringement of a title. These policies may also cover the costs of defending a lawsuit, including attorneys' fees and court costs.

TIP   The comprehensive general liability insurance policies that most business firms carry do not cover the kinds of claims addressed in this book. A special kind of policy known as a *media perils policy* must be obtained to protect you against intellectual property and libel claims.

13.1 Have the Publisher Name You as an "Additional Insured" Party

Most major publishing companies have an umbrella media risks insurance policy applicable to all of their books. Authors should always ask their publishers to name them as an *additional insured* party on the publisher's policy. In this way, the publisher's policy will cover the author personally. While major book publishers routinely cover authors on their insurance policies, other types of publishers—such as magazine and newspaper publishers, as well as small presses and academic presses—may not.

Even when your publisher will agree to name you as an additional insured, you may not be sufficiently protected by the publisher's insurance policy. This is because most major publishers have a significant deductible on their insurance policies. Therefore, it is always important to find out the amount of the deductible on your publisher's policy. If you are unable or unwilling to bear that cost, you may want to obtain your own author's liability policy to cover the shortfall or the deductible amount. You should also inquire whether the deductible applies separately to each individual claimant (e.g., author, publisher, distributor) or whether the deductible applies to each occurrence (i.e., a single deductible for all claimants arising from the publication of a single work).

As of this writing, the Author's Guild provides an author's policy for its members. Several private insurance companies serving the publishing industry also provide co-insurance policies for authors to cover the amount of a publisher's deductible. The costs, terms, and availability of these policies are constantly changing, so it is best to speak with a media insurance broker to find the best policy for your project.

13.2   Look for Adequate Coverage in an Insurance Policy

Insurance policies vary widely. When obtaining an insurance policy, you always need to ask the following questions.

13.2.1   Does the Policy Cover Attorneys' Fees?

Always find out whether the policy will provide coverage for legal fees and defense costs in addition to payment of a damage award. Some policies cover only the cost of a judgment or award, or they limit the coverage for attorneys' fees to a certain amount. Other policies require you to obtain approval before incurring any attorneys' fees or expenses. In addition, it is a good idea to find out whether the policy requires the insurance company to defend a lawsuit against you. If it does, the insurance company has to provide a lawyer to defend you in lawsuits. This can save you a lot of money in legal fees.

13.2.2   Does the Policy Cover Punitive Damages?

Another key point to investigate is whether the insurance policy covers punitive or exemplary damage awards. Some states, such as New York, do not permit insurance companies to insure you against punitive damages. Because an award of punitive damages may be substantial (sometimes even more than actual damages and attorneys' fees), where permissible, you should make sure that your insurance policy covers punitive damages.

13.2.3 Does the Policy Require a Lawyer's Opinion?

Most insurers will not issue a media risks policy unless the author provides an opinion letter from a publishing lawyer analyzing the risks of a lawsuit. Find out whether you will need to provide such a legal opinion letter, because the cost of hiring a lawyer to review your manuscript and to write an opinion letter for the insurance company can be significant. The cost of obtaining the legal review and opinion should also be taken into account when comparing policies and their rates.

13.2.4 What Types of Claims Are Covered?

It is important to speak with the insurance broker to find out exactly which types of claims are covered and which are not. For example, some policies cover claims of intentional infliction of emotional distress or misappropriation of ideas, while others do not. Other insurance policies offer optional coverage, for an additional fee, for claims for bodily injury or property damage resulting from negligent advice or instructions.

All writers should obtain a policy that covers, at a minimum, claims of libel, slander, invasion of privacy, invasion of the right of publicity, trademark and copyright infringement, and unfair competition. Obviously, the more types of claims covered, the better the policy. Many insurance policies exclude certain claims, such as those alleging intentional or malicious acts, from coverage. It is important to find out what types of claims are excluded. You will have to bear the cost of defending these claims yourself.

13.2.5 Which Versions of Your Work Are Covered?

You should investigate whether the insurance policy will cover different versions of a work. If a book will be published in hardcover and paperback forms, make sure the insurance policy will cover both versions. Additionally, find out whether the policy covers condensed versions and serializations of your work. Similarly, you should find out if coverage extends to book jackets, flap copy, press releases, advertising and promotional materials, and personal appearances by the author.

13.2.6   Where Is the Policy Effective?

It may seem like a simple question, but many policyholders fail to ask whether their policy covers claims outside the United States. Many insurance policies only cover claims brought in the United States. If your work is going to be distributed outside of the United States, you'd better make sure that your insurance policy will cover worldwide claims and lawsuits.

13.2.7   Is the Policy a "Claims Made" or an "Occurrence" Policy?

There are two types of insurance policies: "claims made" policies and "occurrence" policies. A *claims made policy* covers claims made during the policy period, whether or not the actual activity that gives rise to the claim occurred before the policy came into effect. An *occurrence policy* covers material published during the policy period. If your policy is a claims made policy, and a lawsuit or claim is brought the day after your policy expires, the insurance policy will *not* cover the claim even though the acts giving rise to the claim occurred while your policy was in effect. Alternatively, with an occurrence policy, it doesn't matter when the claim is made.

13.3   *Insurance Policy Prices*

The premiums for media insurance policies and authors' insurance policies vary, depending on the nature of the work and the likelihood of a claim. The premiums generally take into consideration several factors, including the following:

- *The nature of the work.*   For example, the premium for a work of science fiction may be less than that for an investigative report or exposé, because there is less likelihood of any libel claims for science fiction.
- *Whether releases and permissions have been obtained.*   Where appropri-

ate permissions and releases have been secured, there is reduced risk of lawsuits.

- *Whether any claims have been threatened or made.* When claims have already been threatened or made against the writer in connection with the work sought to be covered by the policy, the risk of a lawsuit skyrockets.
- *The amount of coverage sought and the amount of the deductible, if any.* As coverage goes up, so do the premiums, but as deductibles go up, premiums go down.

CHECKLIST: Media Perils Insurance

- ☐ What types of claims are covered?
- ☐ What is the period of coverage?
- ☐ What is the deductible, and what are the limits of coverage for each claim?
- ☐ Are legal fees and defense costs covered separately or in addition to the maximum policy coverage?
- ☐ What are the conditions for coverage (i.e., are a prepublication review and an opinion letter by an attorney required?)?
- ☐ Who is covered (publisher, author, or both)?
- ☐ Is there an additional charge or fee for naming an author as an additional insured party?
- ☐ Are lawsuits outside the United States covered?
- ☐ Is the policy a "claims made" policy or an "occurrence" policy?
- ☐ Does the policy cover translations or other editions of the work (i.e., mass market paperback, trade paperback, special editions, electronic editions, etc.)?
- ☐ Are punitive damages covered?
- ☐ Do you have the right to have your own attorney represent you, or does the insurance company require its own attorney?
- ☐ Can the insurance company settle a case without your approval, or do you have the right to approve all settlements?
- ☐ Does the policy extend to directors, officers, and employees?

Appendix A

How to Investigate the Copyright Status of a Work (U.S. Copyright Circular R22)

IN GENERAL

Methods of Approaching a Copyright Investigation

There are several ways to investigate whether a work is under copyright protection and, if so, the facts of the copyright. These are the main ones:

1. Examine a copy of the work for such elements as a copyright notice, place and date of publication, author and publisher. If the work is a sound recording, examine the disk, tape cartridge, or cassette in which the recorded sound is fixed, or the album cover, sleeve, or container in which the recording is sold.
2. Make a search of the Copyright Office catalogs and other records; or
3. Have the Copyright Office make a search for you.

A Few Words of Caution About Copyright Investigations

Copyright investigations often involve more than one of these methods. Even if you follow all three approaches, the results may not be conclusive. Moreover, as explained in this circular, the changes brought about under the Copyright Act of 1976, the Berne Convention Implementation Act of 1988, and the Copyright Renewal Act of 1992 must be considered when investigating the copyright status of a work.

This circular offers some practical guidance on what to look for if you are making a copyright investigation. It is important to realize, however, that this circular contains only general information and that there are a number of exceptions to the principles outlined here. In many cases it is important to consult with a copyright attorney before reaching any conclusions regarding the copyright status of a work.

HOW TO SEARCH COPYRIGHT OFFICE CATALOGS AND RECORDS

Catalog of Copyright Entries

The Copyright Office published the *Catalog of Copyright Entries (CCE)* in printed format from 1891 through 1978. From 1979 through 1982 the CCE was issued in microfiche format. The catalog was divided into parts according to the classes of works registered. Each CCE segment covered all registrations made during a particular period of time. Renewal registrations made from 1979 through 1982 are found in Section 8 of the catalog. Renewals prior to that time were generally listed at the end of the volume containing the class of work to which they pertained.

A number of libraries throughout the United States maintain copies of the *Catalog,* and this may provide a good starting point if you wish to make a search yourself. There are some cases, however, in which a search of the *Catalog* alone will not be sufficient to provide the needed information. For example:

- Since the *Catalog* does not include entries for assignments or other recorded documents, it cannot be used for searches involving the ownership of rights.
- The *Catalog* entry contains the essential facts concerning a registration, but it is not a verbatim transcript of the registration record. It does not contain the address of the copyright claimant.

Effective with registrations made since 1982, the only method of searching outside the Library of Congress is by using the

Internet to access the automated catalog. The automated catalog contains entries from 1978 forward. See page 4 for accessing the catalog via the Internet.

Individual Searches of Copyright Records

The Copyright Office is located in the Library of Congress James Madison Memorial Building, 101 Independence Ave., S.E., Washington, D.C. 20559-6000.

Most records of the Copyright Office are open to public inspection and searching from 8:30 a.m. to 5 p.m., Eastern Time, Monday–Friday, except Federal holidays. The various records freely available to the public include an extensive card catalog, an automated catalog containing records from 1978 forward, record books, and microfilm records of assignments and related documents. Other records, including correspondence files and deposit copies, are not open to the public for searching. However, they may be inspected upon request and payment of a $20-per-hour search fee.

If you wish to do your own searching in the Copyright Office files open to the public, you will be given assistance in locating the records you need and in learning procedures for searching. If the Copyright Office staff actually makes the search for you, a search fee must be charged. The search will not be done while you wait.

In addition, the following files dating from 1978 forward are now available over the Internet: COHM, which includes all material except serials and documents; COHD, which includes documents; and COHS, which includes serials.

The Internet site addresses for the Copyright Office files are:

World Wide Web URL: **http://lcweb.loc.gov/copyright**

Gopher: **marvel.loc.gov**

Telnet: **locis.log.gov**

The Copyright Office does **not** offer search assistance to users on the Internet.

SEARCHING BY THE COPYRIGHT OFFICE

In General

Upon request, the Copyright Office staff will search its records at the statutory rate of $20 for each hour or fraction of an hour consumed. Based on the information you furnish, we will provide an estimate of the total search fee. If you decide to have the Office staff conduct the search, you should send the estimated amount with your request. The Office will then proceed with the search and send you a typewritten report or, if you prefer, an oral report by telephone. If you request an oral report, please provide a telephone number where you can be reached during normal business hours 8:30 a.m.–5 p.m. Eastern Time.

Search reports can be certified on request for an extra fee of $20. Certified searches are most frequently requested to meet the evidentiary requirements of litigation.

Your request and any other correspondence should be addressed to:

Reference and Bibliography Section, LM-451
Copyright Office
Library of Congress
Washington, D.C. 20559-6000

Tel: (202) 707-6850
Fax: (202) 707-6859
TTY: (202) 707-6737

What the Fee Does Not Cover

The search fee does **not** include the cost of additional certificates, photocopies of deposits, or copies of other Office records. For information concerning these services, request Circular 6, "Obtaining Access to and Copies of Copyright Office Records and Deposits."

Information Needed

The more detailed information you can furnish with your request, the less time-consuming and expensive the search will be. Please provide as much of the following information as possible:

- The title of the work, with any possible variants;
- The names of the authors, including possible pseudonyms;
- The name of the probable copyright owner, which may be the publisher or producer;
- The approximate year when the work was published or registered;
- The type of work involved (book, play, musical composition, sound recording, photograph, etc.);

- For a work originally published as a part of a periodical or collection, the title of that publication and any other information, such as the volume or issue number, to help identify it;
- Motion pictures are often based on other works such as books or serialized contributions to periodicals or other composite works. **If you desire a search for an underlying work or for music from a motion picture, you must specifically request such a search. You must also identify the underlying works and music and furnish the specific titles, authors, and approximate dates of these works;** and
- The registration number or any other copyright data.

Searches Involving Assignments and Other Documents Affecting Copyright Ownership

The Copyright Office staff will also, for the standard hourly search fee, search its indexes covering the records of assignments and other recorded documents concerning ownership of copyrights. The reports of searches in these cases will state the facts shown in the Office's indexes of the recorded documents but will offer no interpretation of the content of the documents or their legal effect.

LIMITATIONS ON SEARCHES

In determining whether or not to have a search made, you should keep the following points in mind:

No Special Lists. The Copyright Office does not maintain any listings of works by subject or any lists of works that are in the public domain.

Contributions Not Listed Separately in Copyright Office Records. Individual works such as stories, poems, articles, or musical compositions that were published as contributions to a copyrighted periodical or collection are usually not listed separately by title in our records.

No Comparisons. The Copyright Office does not search or compare copies of works to determine questions of possible infringement or to determine how much two or more versions of a work have in common.

Titles and Names Not Copyrightable. Copyright does not protect names and titles,

and our records list many different works identified by the same or similar titles. Some brand names, trade names, slogans, and phrases may be entitled to protection under the general rules of law relating to unfair competition. They may also be entitled to registration under the provisions of the trademark laws. Questions about the trademark laws should be addressed to the Commissioner of Patents and Trademarks, Washington, D.C. 20231. Possible protection of names and titles under common law principles of unfair competition is a question of state law.

No Legal Advice. The Copyright Office cannot express any opinion as to the legal significance or effect of the facts included in a search report.

SOME WORDS OF CAUTION

Searches Not Always Conclusive

Searches of the Copyright Office catalogs and records are useful in helping to determine the copyright status of a work, but they cannot be regarded as conclusive in all cases. The complete absence of any information about a work in the Office records does not mean that the work is unprotected. The following are examples of cases in which information about a particular work may be incomplete or lacking entirely in the Copyright Office:

- Before 1978, unpublished works were entitled to protection under common law without the need of registration.
- Works published with notice prior to 1978 may be registered at **any** time within the first 28-year term.
- Works copyrighted between January 1, 1964, and December 31, 1977, are affected by the Copyright Renewal Act of 1992 which automatically extends the copyright term and makes renewal registrations optional.
- For works under copyright protection on or after January 1, 1978, registration may be made at any time during the term of protection. Although registration is not required as a condition of copyright protection, there are certain definite advantages to registration. For further information, request Circular 1, "Copyright Basics."
- Since searches are ordinarily limited to registrations that have already been cata-

loged, a search report may not cover recent registrations for which catalog records are not yet available.

- The information in the search request may not have been complete or specific enough to identify the work.
- The work may have been registered under a different title or as part of a larger work.

Protection in Foreign Countries

Even if you conclude that a work is in the public domain in the United States, this does not necessarily mean that you are free to use it in other countries. Every nation has its own laws governing the length and scope of copyright protection, and these are applicable to uses of the work within that nation's borders. Thus, the expiration or loss of copyright protection in the United States may still leave the work fully protected against unauthorized use in other countries.

OTHER CIRCULARS

For further information, request Circular 6, "Obtaining Access to and Copies of Copyright Office Records and Deposits"; Circular 15, "Renewal of Copyright"; Circular 15a, "Duration of Copyright"; and Circular 15t, "Extension of Copyright Terms," from:

> Publications Section, LM-455
> Copyright Office
> Library of Congress
> Washington, D.C. 20559-6000

You may call (202) 707-9100 at any time, day or night, to leave a request for forms or circulars as a recorded message on the Forms HOTLINE. Requests made on the HOTLINE number are filled and mailed promptly.

IMPACT OF COPYRIGHT ACT ON COPYRIGHT INVESTIGATIONS

On October 19, 1976, the President signed into law a complete revision of the copyright law of the United States (Title 17 of the United States Code). Most provisions of this statute came into force on January 1, 1978, superseding the copyright act of 1909. These provisions made significant changes in the copyright law. Further important changes resulted from the Berne Convention Implementation Act of 1988, which took ef-

fect March 1, 1989, and the Copyright Renewal Act of 1992 (P.L. 102-307) enacted June 26, 1992, which amended the renewal provisions of the copyright law. If you need more information about the provisions of either the 1909 or the 1976 law, write or call the Copyright Office. For information about the Berne Convention Implementation Act, request Circular 93, "Highlights of U.S. Adherence to the Berne Convention." For information about renewals, request Circular 15, "Renewal of Copyright." For single copies of the law only, request Circular 92, "Copyright Law of the United States of America," from:

> Publications Section, LM 455
> Copyright Office
> Library of Congress
> Washington, D.C. 20559-6000

For multiple copies of the law, request "Copyright Law, Circular 92" $4.75 each, stock number 030-002-00182-9 from:

> New Orders
> Superintendent of Documents
> P.O. Box 371954
> Pittsburgh, PA 15250-7954

> Tel: (202) 783-3238
> Fax: (202) 512-2250

For copyright investigations, the following points about the impact of the Copyright Act of 1976, the Berne Convention Implementation Act of 1988, and the Copyright Renewal Act of 1992 should be considered:

A Changed System of Copyright Formalities

Some of the most sweeping changes under the 1976 Act involve copyright formalities, that is, the procedural requirements for securing and maintaining full copyright protection. The old system of formalities involved copyright notice, deposit and registration, recordation of transfers and licenses of copyright ownership, and United States manufacture, among other things. In general, while retaining formalities, the 1976 law reduced the chances of mistakes, softened the consequences of errors and omissions, and allowed for the correction of errors.

The Berne Convention Implementation Act of 1988 reduced formalities, most notably making the addition of the previously mandatory copyright notice optional. It should be noted that the amended notice requirements are not retroactive.

The Copyright Renewal Act of 1992, enacted June 26, 1992, automatically extends the term of copyrights secured between January 1, 1964, and December 31, 1977, making renewal registration optional. Consult Circular 15, "Renewal of Copyright," for details. For additional information, you may contact the Renewals Section.

Tel: (202) 707-8180
Fax: (202) 707-3849

Automatic Copyright

Under the present copyright law, copyright exists in original works of authorship created and fixed in any tangible medium of expression, now known or later developed, from which they can be perceived, reproduced, or otherwise communicated, either directly, or indirectly with the aid of a machine or device. In other words, copyright is an incident of creative authorship not dependent on statutory formalities. Thus, registration with the Copyright Office generally is not required, but there are certain advantages that arise from a timely registration. For further information on the advantages of registration, write or call the Copyright Office and request Circular 1, "Copyright Basics."

Copyright Notice

The 1909 Copyright Act and, as originally enacted, the 1976 Copyright Act required a notice of copyright on published works. For most works, a copyright notice consisted of the symbol ©, the word "Copyright," or the abbreviation "Copr.," together with the name of the owner of copyright and the year of first publication. For example: "© Joan Crane 1994" or "Copyright 1994 by Abraham Adams."

For sound recordings published on or after February 15, 1972, a copyright notice might read "℗1994 XYZ Records, Inc." See below for more information about sound recordings.

For mask works, a copyright notice might read "Ⓜ SDR Industries." Request Circular 100, "Federal Statutory Protection for Mask Works," for more information.

As originally enacted, the 1976 law prescribed that all visually perceptible published copies of a work, or published phonorecords of a sound recording, should bear a proper copyright notice. This applies to such works published before March 1, 1989. After March 1, 1989, notice of copyright on these works is optional. Adding the notice, however, is strongly encouraged and, if litigation involving the copyright occurs, certain advantages exist for publishing a work with notice.

Prior to March 1, 1989, the requirement for the notice applied equally whether the work was published in the United States or elsewhere by authority of the copyright owner. Compliance with the statutory notice requirements was the responsibility of the copyright owner. Unauthorized publication without the copyright notice, or with a defective notice, does not affect the validity of the copyright in the work.

Advance permission from, or registration with, the Copyright Office is not required before placing a copyright notice on copies of the work or on phonorecords of a sound recording. Moreover, for works first published on or after January 1, 1978, through February 28, 1989, omission of the required notice, or use of a defective notice, did not result in forfeiture or outright loss of copyright protection. Certain omissions of, or defects in, the notice of copyright, however, could have led to loss of copyright protection if steps were not taken to correct or cure the omissions or defects. The Copyright Office has issued a final regulation (37 CFR 201.20) which suggests various acceptable positions for the notice of copyright. For further information, write to the Copyright Office and request Circular 3, "Copyright Notice," and Circular 96, Section 201.20, "Methods of Affixation and Positions of the Copyright Notice on Various Types of Works."

Works Already in the Public Domain

Neither the 1976 Act, the Berne Convention Implementation Act of 1988, nor the Copyright Renewal Act of 1992 will restore protection to works that fell into the public domain before the passage of the laws. However, the North American Free Trade Agreement Implementation Act (NAFTA) and the Uruguay Round Agreements Act (URAA) may restore copyright in certain works of foreign origin that were in the public domain in the United States. Under the copyright law in effect prior to January 1, 1978, copyright could be lost in several situations. The most common were publication without the required notice of copyright, expiration of the first 28-year term without renewal, or final expiration of the second copyright term. The Copyright Renewal Act of 1992 automatically renews first term copyrights secured between January 1, 1964 and December 31, 1977.

Scope of Exclusive Rights Under Copyright

The present law has changed and enlarged in some cases the scope of the copyright owner's rights. The new rights apply to all uses of a work subject to protection by copyright after January 1, 1978, regardless of when the work was created.

DURATION OF COPYRIGHT PROTECTION

Works Originally Copyrighted On or After January 1, 1978

A work that is created and fixed in tangible form for the first time on or after January 1, 1978, is automatically protected from the moment of its creation and is ordinarily given a term enduring for the author's life plus an additional 50 years after the author's death. In the case of "a joint work prepared by two or more authors who did not work for hire," the term lasts for 50 years after the last surviving author's death. For works made for hire and for anonymous and pseudonymous works (unless the author's identity is revealed in the Copyright Office records), the duration of copyright will be 75 years from publication or 100 years from creation, whichever is less.

Works created before the 1976 law came into effect but neither published nor registered for copyright before January 1, 1978, have been automatically brought under the statute and are now given Federal copyright protection. The duration of copyright in these works will generally be computed in the same way as for new works: the life-plus-50 or 75/100-year terms will apply. However, all works in this category are guaranteed at least 25 years of statutory protection.

Works Copyrighted Before January 1, 1978

Under the law in effect before 1978, copyright was secured either on the date a work was published with notice of copyright or on the date of registration if the work was registered in unpublished form. In either case, copyright endured for a first term of 28 years from the date on which it was secured. During the last (28th) year of the first term, the copyright was eligible for renewal. The 1976 copyright law extended the renewal term from 28 to 47 years for copyrights in existence on January 1, 1978.

However, for works copyrighted prior to January 1, 1964, the copyright still must have been renewed in the 28th calendar year to receive the 47-year period of added protection. The amending legislation enacted June 26, 1992, automatically extends this second term for works first copyrighted between January 1, 1964, and December 31, 1977. For more detailed information on the copyright term, write or call the Copyright Office and request Circular 15a, "Duration of Copyright," and Circular 15t, "Extension of Copyright Terms."

WORKS FIRST PUBLISHED BEFORE 1978: THE COPYRIGHT NOTICE

General Information About the Copyright Notice

In investigating the copyright status of works first published before January 1, 1978, the most important thing to look for is the notice of copyright. As a general rule under the previous law, copyright protection was lost permanently if the notice was omitted from the first authorized published edition of a work or if it appeared in the wrong form or position. The form and position of the copyright notice for various types of works were specified in the copyright statute. Some courts were liberal in overlooking relatively minor departures from the statutory requirements, but a basic failure to comply with the notice provisions forfeited copyright protection and put the work into the public domain in this country.

Absence of Copyright Notice

For works published before 1978, the complete absence of a copyright notice from a published copy generally indicates that the work is not protected by copyright. For works first published before March 1, 1989, the copyright notice is mandatory, but omission could have been cured by registration before or within 5 years of publication and by adding the notice to copies published in the United States after discovery of the omission. Some works may contain a notice, others may not. The absence of a notice in works published on or after March 1, 1989, does not necessarily indicate that the work is in the public domain.

Unpublished Works. No notice of copyright was required on the copies of any unpublished work. The concept of "publication" is very technical, and it was possible for a number of copies lacking a copyright notice to be reproduced and distributed without affecting copyright protection.

Foreign Editions. In the case of works seeking *ad interim* copyright,* copies of a copyrighted work were exempted from the notice requirements if they were first published outside the United States. Some copies of these foreign editions could find their way into the United States without impairing the copyright.

Accidental Omission. The 1909 statute preserved copyright protection if the notice was omitted by accident or mistake from a "particular copy or copies."

Unauthorized Publication. A valid copyright was not secured if someone deleted the notice and/or published the work without authorization from the copyright owner.

Sound Recordings. Reproductions of sound recordings usually contain two different types of creative works: the underlying musical, dramatic, or literary work that is being performed or read and the fixation of the actual sounds embodying the performance or reading. For protection of the underlying musical or literary work embodied in a recording, it is not necessary that a copyright notice covering this material appear on the phonograph records or tapes on which the recording is reproduced. As noted above, a special notice is required for protection of the recording of a series of musical, spoken, or other sounds which were fixed on or after February 15, 1972. Sound recordings fixed before February 15, 1972, are not eligible for Federal copyright protection. The Sound Recording Act of 1971, the present copyright law, and the Berne Convention Implementation Act of 1988 cannot be applied or be construed to provide any retroactive protection for sound recordings fixed before February 15, 1972. Such works, however, may be protected by various state laws or doctrines of common law.

The Date in the Copyright Notice

If you find a copyright notice, the date it contains may be important in determining the

copyright status of the work. In general, the notice on works published before 1978 must include the year in which copyright was secured by publication or, if the work was first registered for copyright in unpublished form, the year in which registration was made. There are two main exceptions to this rule.

1. For pictorial, graphic, or sculptural works (Classes F through K under the 1909 law), the law permitted omission of the year date in the notice.
2. For "new versions" of previously published or copyrighted works, the notice was not usually required to include more than the year of first publication of the new version itself. This is explained further under "Derivative Works" below.

The year in the notice usually (though not always) indicated when the copyright began. It is therefore significant in determining whether a copyright is still in effect; or, if the copyright has not yet run its course, the year date will help in deciding when the copyright is scheduled to expire. For further information about the duration of copyright, request Circular 15a, "Duration of Copyright."

In evaluating the meaning of the date in a notice, you should keep the following points in mind:

WORKS PUBLISHED AND COPYRIGHTED BEFORE JANUARY 1, 1978: A work published before January 1, 1978, and copyrighted within the past 75 years may still be protected by copyright in the United States if a valid renewal registration was made during the 28th year of the first term of the copyright. If renewed by registration or under the Copyright Renewal Act of 1992 and if still valid under the other provisions of the law, the copyright will expire 75 years from the end of the year in which it was first secured.

Therefore, the United States copyright in any work published or copyrighted more than 75 years ago (75 years from January 1st in the present year) has expired by operation of law, and the work has permanently fallen into the public domain in the United States. For example, on January 1, 1995, copyright in works first published or copyrighted before January 1, 1920, have expired; on January 1, 1996, copyright in works first published or copyrighted before January 1, 1921, will have expired.

WORKS FIRST PUBLISHED OR COPYRIGHTED BETWEEN JANUARY 1, 1920,

---

*"*Ad interim* copyright" refers to a special short term of copyright available to certain pre-1978 books and periodicals. For further information on *ad interim* copyright, see page 10.

AND DECEMBER 31, 1949, BUT NOT RENEWED: If a work was first published or copyrighted between January 1, 1920, and December 31, 1949, it is important to determine whether the copyright was renewed during the last (28th) year of the first term of the copyright. This can be done by searching the Copyright Office records or catalogs as explained above. If no renewal registration was made, copyright protection expired permanently at the end of the 28th year of the year date it was first secured.

WORKS FIRST PUBLISHED OR COPYRIGHTED BETWEEN JANUARY 1, 1920, AND DECEMBER 31, 1949, AND REGISTERED FOR RENEWAL: When a valid renewal registration was made and copyright in the work was in its second term on December 31, 1977, the renewal copyright term was extended under the present act to 47 years. In these cases, copyright will last for a total of 75 years from the end of the year in which copyright was originally secured. Example: Copyright in a work first published in 1920 and renewed in 1948 will expire on December 31, 1995.

WORKS FIRST PUBLISHED OR COPYRIGHTED BETWEEN JANUARY 1, 1950, AND DECEMBER 31, 1963: If a work was in its first 28-year term of copyright protection on January 1, 1978, it must have been renewed in a timely fashion to have secured the maximum term of copyright protection. If renewal registration was made during the 28th calendar year of its first term, copyright would endure for 75 years from the end of the year copyright was originally secured. If not renewed, the copyright expired at the end of its 28th calendar year.

WORKS FIRST PUBLISHED OR COPYRIGHTED BETWEEN JANUARY 1, 1964, AND DECEMBER 31, 1977: If a work was in its first 28-year term of copyright protection on June 26, 1992, renewal registration is now optional. The term of copyright for works published or copyrighted during this time period has been extended to 75 years by the Copyright Renewal Act of 1992. There is no need to make the renewal filing in order to extend the original 28-year copyright term to the full 75 years.

However, there are several advantages to making a renewal registration during the 28th year of the original term of copyright. If renewal registration is made during the 28th year of the original term of copyright, the renewal copyright vests in the name of the renewal claimant on the effective date of the renewal registration; the renewal certificate constitutes *prima facie* evidence as to the validity of the copyright during the renewed and extended term and of the facts stated in the certificate; and, the right to use the derivative work in the extended term may be affected. Request Circular 15, "Renewal of Copyright," for further information.

UNPUBLISHED, UNREGISTERED WORKS: Before 1978, if a work had been neither "published" in the legal sense nor registered in the Copyright Office, it was subject to perpetual protection under the common law. On January 1, 1978, all works of this kind, subject to protection by copyright, were automatically brought under the Federal copyright statute. The duration of copyright for these works can vary, but none of them will expire before December 31, 2002.

Derivative Works

In examining a copy (or a record, disk, or tape) for copyright information, it is important to determine whether that particular version of the work is an original edition of the work or a "new version." New versions include musical arrangements, adaptations, revised or newly edited editions, translations, dramatizations, abridgments, compilations, and works republished with new matter added. The law provides that derivative works, published or unpublished, are independently copyrightable and that the copyright in such a work does not affect or extend the protection, if any, in the underlying work. Under the 1909 law, courts have also held that the notice of copyright on a derivative work ordinarily need not include the dates or other information pertaining to the earlier works incorporated in it. This principle is specifically preserved in the present copyright law. Thus, if the copy (or the record, disk, or tape) constitutes a derivative version of the work, these points should be kept in mind:

- The date in the copyright notice is not necessarily an indication of when copyright in all of the material in the work will expire. Some of the material may already be in the public domain, and some parts of the work may expire sooner than others.
- Even if some of the material in the derivative work is in the public domain and free for use, this does not mean that the "new" material added to it can be used without

permission from the owner of copyright in the derivative work. It may be necessary to compare editions to determine what is free to use and what is not.

- Ownership of rights in the material included in a derivative work and in the preexisting work upon which it may be based may differ, and permission obtained from the owners of certain parts of the work may not authorize the use of other parts.

The Name in the Copyright Notice

Under the copyright statute in effect before 1978, the notice was required to include "the name of the copyright proprietor." The present act requires that the notice include "the name of the owner of copyright in the work, or an abbreviation by which the name can be recognized, or a generally known alternative designation of the owner." The name in the notice (sometimes in combination with the other statements on the copy, records, disk, tape, container, or label) often gives persons wishing to use the work the information needed to identify the owner from whom licenses or permission can be sought. In other cases, the name provides a starting point for a search in the Copyright Office records or catalogs, as explained at the beginning in this circular.

In the case of works published before 1978, copyright registration is made in the name of the individual person or the entity identified as the copyright owner in the notice. For works published on or after January 1, 1978, registration is made in the name of the person or entity owning all the rights on the date the registration is made. This may or may not be the name appearing in the notice. In addition to its records of copyright registration, the Copyright Office maintains extensive records of assignments, exclusive licenses, and other documents dealing with copyright ownership.

Ad Interim

Ad interim copyright was a special short-term copyright that applied to certain books and periodicals in the English language that were first manufactured and published outside the United States. It was a partial exception to the manufacturing requirements of the previous United States copyright law. Its purpose was to secure temporary United States protection for a work, pending the manufacture of an edition in the United States. The *ad interim* requirements changed several times over the years and were subject to a number of exceptions and qualifications.

The manufacturing provisions of the copyright act expired on July 1, 1986, and are no longer a part of the copyright law. The transitional and supplementary provisions of the act provide that for any work in which *ad interim* copyright was subsisting or capable of being secured on December 31, 1977, copyright protection would be extended for a term compatible with the other works in which copyright was subsisting on the effective date of the new act. Consequently, if the work was first published on or after July 1, 1977, and was eligible for *ad interim* copyright protection, the provisions of the present copyright act will be applicable to the protection of these works. Anyone investigating the copyright status of an English-language book or periodical first published outside the United States before July 1, 1977, should check carefully to determine:

- Whether the manufacturing requirements were applicable to the work; and
- If so, whether the *ad interim* requirements were met.

What's New Online at the U.S. Copyright Office

Fax-on-Demand Supplies Circulars and Announcements

Frequently requested Copyright Office circulars and announcements are now available via fax. Call **202-707-2600** from any touchtone telephone. Key in your fax number at the prompt and the document number of the item(s) you want to receive by fax. The item(s) will be transmitted to your fax machine. If you do not know the document number of the item(s) you want, you may request that a menu be faxed to you. You may order up to three items at a time. Note that copyright application forms are *not* available by fax.

All U.S. Copyright Application Forms Available on Internet

All U.S. Copyright Office application forms are now available on the Internet. They may be downloaded and printed for use in registering a claim to copyright or for use in renewing a claim to copyright. In addition, the format for filing a Notice of Intent to Enforce (NIE) a copyright restored under the Uruguay Round Agreements Act (URAA) is also available on the Internet.

The forms and the format may be accessed and downloaded by connecting to the Library of Congress home page on the Wide World Web (WWW) and selecting the copyright link.

The address is:
http://www.loc.gov

Or you may connect through the Copyright Office home page.

The address is:
http://www.loc.gov/copyright

You must have Adobe® Acrobat® Reader installed on your computer to view and print the forms. The free Adobe® Acrobat® Reader may be downloaded from Adobe Systems Incorporated through links from the same Internet site at which the forms are available.

Print forms head to head (top of page 2 is directly behind the top of page 1) on a single piece of good quality, 8.5-inch by 11-inch paper. To achieve the best quality copies of the application forms, use a laser printer.

Copyright Office Publications Available Over the Internet

Frequently requested Copyright Office circulars, announcements, and recently proposed as well as final regulations are now available over the Internet. These documents may be examined and downloaded through the Library of Congress campus-wide information systems LC MARVEL.

Connect to LC MARVEL via gopher at marvel.loc.gov (port 70) or through the WWW addresses above. The WWW addresses give you access to information created by the Copyright Office and links to other copyright resources created elsewhere. Effective October 2, 1995, the Library of Congress no longer supports telnet access to LC MARVEL.

Copyright Office Files Available Over the Internet

Copyright Office records in machine-readable form cataloged from Jan. 1, 1978, to the present including registration information and recorded documents are now available over the Internet. These include the following files; **COHM**, which contains all original and renewal registrations except serials; **COHD**, which contains documents; and **COHS**, which contains serials. These files may be examined through LOCIS (Library of Congress Information System). You can connect to LOCIS directly by using telnet, or you can also reach LOCIS through the Library of Congress gopher LC MARVEL and the World Wide Web.

The WWW address is:
http://www.loc.gov/copyright

The gopher address is:
marvel.loc.gov
port 70

The telnet address is:
locis.loc.gov

Internet Access Information

When:
LC MARVEL and WWW are available 24 hours a day. LOCIS is available 24 hours a day Monday–Friday, eastern time; Saturday, until 5 p.m.; Sunday, after 11 a.m.* If you have trouble connecting to LOCIS, it may be because of the limit on the number of simultaneous connections permitted or because your Internet service provider or the browser or client software you are using does not support the telnet or tn3270 function.

Cost:
The Library of Congress and the Copyright Office charge no fees to connect to their Internet resources.

Search Assistance:
The Copyright Office *does not* offer search assistance to users of the Internet.

*Not all files are available after 9:30 p.m. on weekdays. On Sundays, all files may not be available from 5 p.m.–8 p.m.

Appendix C

Sample Forms

Form A: *Permission Request Letter*

[Date]

[Company Name]

[Company Address]

Attn.:   Permissions Department

Re: Permission Request

My Reference No. [insert your manuscript page no.]

Dear Sir or Madam:

I would like to obtain permission to use the following material for a book I am preparing for [name of publisher], the details of which are as follows:

[Proposed Usage]

Tentative Title of Work: _____

Author[s]: _____

Publisher: _____

Publication Date: _____

Tentative Price: _____

Initial Print Run: _____

Format/Medium: [e.g., 176 pages, trade paperback] [if seeking electronic rights, specify which electronic medium you require] _____

[Rights Sought]

[Option 1: Broad Grant of Rights] "the nonexclusive right to include the following material in this and all subsequent editions of my book, in all foreign language translations and other derivative works published or prepared by me, or my successors, assigns, or licensees, for distribution throughout the world."

[Option 2: Narrower Grant of Rights] "the nonexclusive right to include the following material in this and all subsequent editions of my book, in English and other derivative works published or prepared by me, or my successors, assigns, or licensees, for distribution throughout [the world] [the United States, its possession, territories, and Canada]." [Strike one out.]

[Material Requested]

Title of Book/Periodical/Journal: _____

Full Name of Author[s]: _____

Volume/Issue/Edition #: _____

Date of Publication [copyright date or issue date]: _____

ISBN [books only]: _____

ISSN [journals/periodicals only]: _____

Beginning on page ___, line ___, with the words _____ .

Ending on page ___, line ___, with the words _____ .

Illustration/Figure No. ___ on page ___ (photocopy attached for ease of reference).

Chart No. ___ on page ___ (photocopy attached for ease of reference).

Kindly grant our request for the aforementioned rights by signing and returning to me a signed copy of this letter. If you do not control rights, or if additional copyright permissions are needed, kindly indicate below whom I should contact.

A self-addressed stamped envelope is enclosed for your convenience.

Thank you.

Sincerely yours,

_____

[Your signature]

_____

[Your name]

_____

[Address]

_____

[Phone/Fax/E-mail]

AGREED AND ACCEPTED:

By: _____
      Authorized signature

Name: _____

Title: _____

Fee: _____   Fee Waived: _____

Credit Line: _____

_____

Copyright Notice: _____

_____

Other Remarks: _____

_____

Form B: Release Form for Interview

[Your Name]   [Date]

[Your Address]

Dear _____,

You have informed me that you are the author of a book tentatively entitled _____ (the "Book") to be published [by Publisher or about subject matter of book].

You have interviewed me for the Book, and I hereby consent to your use of my name, photographs, comments as quoted or derived from the interview(s), and any materials I provided to you, in the publication, advertising, or promotion of the Book, and any editions or revisions thereof, in any languages, throughout the world. I hereby consent to your use of my name, likeness, and biography and the right to fictionalize same, and to portray, impersonate, or simulate me in any way whatsoever, and to make use of any incidents or episodes in my life, factually, fictionally, or in any combination thereof, in preparation, production, performance, broadcast, exhibition, and exploitation of one or more motion pictures or television programs, or both, including episodes of any television series (herein collectively referred to as the "program"), including, but not limited to, merchandising, publication, and other allied rights therein. You shall have the right to use the proceeds of any interviews in and in connection with the Book, and all services rendered by me hereunder (including my interviews and conversations) are rendered as a "work for hire" for copyright purposes.

I understand that the Book and/or portions thereof may be published in newspapers, magazines, and other printed media and may be released or distributed in other recorded media, such as television, motion pictures, computer disk, videodisc, and by other electronic means. I hereby consent to all such derivative uses, including the exhibition and publication in any and all media, now known or hereafter discovered throughout the world in perpetuity. Rights granted herein may be assigned to other individuals or entities.

I waive any right to inspect the Book or program(s). I further waive any claim in connection with the aforementioned use or uses, including, but not limited to, claims relating to defamation, rights of privacy or publicity, confidentiality, copyright, or otherwise.

I represent and warrant that I have full right, power, and authority to execute this Agreement, and I am over twnety-one years of age.

Very truly yours,

_____

[Interviewee's signature]

_____

[Interviewee's name]

_____

[Address]

_____

[Telephone]

Form C: *Release Form for Interview (Another Form)*

For valuable consideration, receipt of which is hereby acknowledged, I hereby grant to [author] and [his/her] licensees, assigns, and successors the right to use all or any part of my statements, or any paraphrase thereof, and/or the right to describe and portray, in whole or in part, me and any events, episodes, or biographical information about me in [his/her] proposed work of [fiction/nonfiction] about [topic], presently entitled [title] in all its subsidiary and derivative publications (the "Work"), and for the advertising and promotion of the Work.

I understand that my name and likeness may or may not be used in the Work and related advertising and promotion, and I consent to the use or nonuse of the same.

I hereby consent to the taping and other recording of any conversations and interviews in which I may participate. [Author] shall have the right to use the results and proceeds of any such conversations and interviews in and in connection with the Work, and all services rendered by me hereunder (including any interviews and conversations) are rendered as a "work made for hire" for copyright purposes.

I agree that I shall have no right, title, or interest in any such material (including the Work) and no claim of any kind whatsoever arising out of such use (including but not limited to any claims of libel, slander, invasion of privacy, invasion of right of publicity, and/or copyright infringement).

(a)   I am over the age of twenty-one. I have read the foregoing and fully understand its contents.

Name: _____   Date: _____

Signature: _____

[If minor, parent or guardian must sign below]

(b)   I represent that I am the parent or guardian of _____,
a minor, and I further warrant that I am of full age and have the legal authority to execute the above release on behalf of said minor. I have read the release before signing it and am fully aware of its contents. This release shall remain binding upon me, our successors, assigns, legal representatives, and heirs.

Name: _____   Date: _____

Signature: _____
                Father/Mother/Legal Guardian

Address: _____

Witness: [Optional] _____

Minor's full name: _____

Minor's address: _____

_____

Form D: Model Release for Photograph

[Date]

For valuable consideration, the receipt and sufficiency of which is hereby acknowledged, I, [name of model], hereby give [name of photographer] the right to photograph me and the irrevocable and perpetual right to use and exploit the photographs that [he/she] has taken of me (in which I may be included with others) in any and all media throughout the world in perpetuity, including but not limited to the following rights:

(a)   The right to copyright the same in [his/her] own name or any other name that [he/she] may choose;

(b)   The right to use, reuse, publish, and republish the same in whole or in part, severally or in conjunction with other photographs and/or text, in any medium and for any purpose whatsoever, including (but not limited to) illustration, promotion, and advertising and trade without any compensation or further compensation to me; and

(c)   The right to use my name in connection therewith if [he/she] so chooses.

I hereby release and discharge [name of photographer] and [his/her] licensees, assigns, and successors from any and all claims and demands arising out of or in connection with the use of the photographs, including but not limited to any and all claims for defamation, invasion of privacy, invasion of right of publicity, and copyright infringement.

This authorization and release shall enure to the benefit of all legal representatives, licensees, and assigns of [name of photographer], as well as the person(s) for whom [he/she] took the photographs.

I have read the foregoing and fully understand the contents thereof.

_____

Signature of model

_____

Print name

_____

Address

_____

Telephone

_____

Date

_____

Witness [Optional]

[If model is a minor, parent or guardian must sign below]

I represent that I am the parent or guardian of the minor whose name appears above. I hereby consent to the foregoing on his/her behalf.

Parent/guardian's name: _____

Signature: _____

Address: _____

Date: _____

Form E: *Nonexclusive Photograph License*

[Date]

To: [Photographer]

[Address]

Dear _____,

This letter shall serve to confirm the agreement pursuant to which [name of author] (the "Author") has acquired the nonexclusive right and license to reproduce, upon the terms and conditions set forth below, the following photographs/artworks (attach additional sheets if necessary):

1.   You hereby grant to Author the following rights with respect to the photographs/artworks:

(a)   The nonexclusive right to reproduce the photographs/artworks in and in conjunction with the book tentatively entitled [title] to be published by [name of publisher] in the English language in the United States of America and Canada (and their territories and possessions) in [hardcover/softcover/or hardcover and softcover] edition(s) and/or on the cover of the book;

(b)   The right to use the photographs/artworks, together with your name and pertinent biographical data in the book and in connection with the advertising and promotion of the book;

(c)   The right to reprint or cause to be reprinted the photographs/artworks in connection with any reprinting, revision, or reproduction of the book in any language and/or medium, whether now known or hereafter devised;

(d)   The right to, and to authorize others to, reprint the photographs/artworks in connection with the inclusion of all or part of the book in any other work in any medium, whether now known or hereafter devised.

2.   You shall deliver to Author copies of the photographs/artworks suitable for reproduction and publication in the book at your own cost and expense. Author shall not be obligated to return the photographs/artworks to you unless you specifically request the return of the photographs/artworks in writing within thirty (30) days from delivery to Author. You shall deliver the photographs/artworks to us no later than [date for delivery].

3.   Any associate or assistant you may retain in connection with furnishing the photographs/artworks shall be at your own cost and expense and will not be deemed to be an agent or employee of Author.

4.   In exchange for this license and the rights granted to Author, Author shall pay to you the sum of $ _____ upon publication of the book.

5.   You represent and warrant that you are the sole author and owner of all rights in and to the photographs/artworks and that the photographs/artworks are original and do not infringe upon any statutory copyright or any common law right or proprietary right of any individual or organization. You shall indemnify Author and hold Author (and its licensees, assigns, and successors) harmless against any and all loss, damages, and/or expenses that we

may suffer by reason of any claim arising from the breach of any of these representations or warranties made by you.

Please confirm that the foregoing accurately and completely sets forth our agreement by signing and returning the enclosed copy hereof.

Very truly yours,

_____

[Your signature]

_____

[Printed or typed name of author]

Confirmed and agreed:

Signature: _____
                [Photographer's signature]

Name: _____
                Print photographer's name

Date: _____

Form F: Property Release

For valuable consideration, receipt of which is hereby acknowledged, I hereby grant [name of photographer], [his/her] successors, assigns, legal representatives, and heirs the right to photograph [full description of property or premises] (the "Property") for purposes of editorial, promotion, advertising or trade, or any other purpose, alone or conjunction with other matter, printed or otherwise, in all forms of media, whether now known or hereinafter invented, without restriction or limitation.

I hereby waive any rights in or approval of the photograph(s), or any manner in which [it/ they] may be used, in part or in whole, without limitation, in connection with any goods or services.

I hereby release and discharge [name of photographer], [his/her] successors, assigns, legal representatives, and heirs, and all persons acting with [his/her] permission or authority, from any liability, including, but not limited to, copyright infringement, trade disparagement, trademark infringement, trademark dilution, and tarnishment, as a result of any distortion, alteration, morphing, or use in composite form, whether produced by standard photographic techniques or by computer, and without restriction, for any purpose whatsoever.

I warrant and represent that I am of legal age and capacity, and I have the authority to enter into this agreement. I have read this release in its entirety prior to signing it, and I am fully familiar with its contents. This agreement shall be binding on me, my agents, employees, successors, assigns, legal representatives, and heirs.

_____

Authorized signature

_____

Name/Title

_____

Address

_____

Date

_____

Witness [Optional]

Form G: Simple "Work Made for Hire" Agreement (Flat Fee)

[Letter Agreement Form with Backup Copyright Assignment]

Dear [Name of contractor]:

This will confirm our understanding regarding certain work we have commissioned you to create, as described below:

[description of independent contractor's contribution or services, e.g., editorial services, indexing, illustrations, or photography] (the "Work").

1. You agree to complete and deliver the Work to us by no later than [date].

2. In consideration for your services as an independent contractor, we shall pay you [amount], according to the following schedule: [schedule of payments]. No further payment shall be due you.

3. We both acknowledge that the material contributed by you, and your services, have been specially ordered by us for use in connection with [title of main work into which contractor's work will be incorporated]. We both agree that your Work shall be considered a "work made for hire," as defined by the copyright laws of the United States. You understand that we shall be the sole and exclusive owner of the Work, including all copyrights to the Work. If for any reason the Work is determined not to be a "work made for hire," you hereby irrevocably transfer and assign to us all right, title, and interest in the Work, including all copyrights, together with all renewals and extensions thereto.

4. You agree to waive any so-called moral rights in the Work.

5. You represent that, except with respect to material furnished to you by us, you are the sole author of the Work, and all of your services are original with you and not copied in whole or in part from any other work; that your Work is not libelous or obscene, and it does not knowingly violate the rights of privacy or publicity, or any other rights of any person, firm, or entity.

6. This agreement shall be governed by the laws of the State of [name of state] and shall be binding upon our successors, assigns, legal representatives, and heirs.

If you agree and accept the aforementioned terms and conditions, please sign below, and return this letter to us.

Sincerely,

_____

[Signature of client or hiring party]

AGREED AND ACCEPTED:

By: _____
    [Authorized signature]

Name: _____
    [Contractor's full name]

Citizenship: _____

Social Security No.: _____
    [Contractor's Social Security Number]

Form H: Short-Form Copyright Assignment

[Note: This is an "All-Rights" transfer of copyright; i.e., Assignor relinquishes all rights under copyright]

FOR GOOD AND VALUABLE CONSIDERATION, receipt of which is hereby acknowledged, [name of assignor] ("Assignor"), located at [address], hereby irrevocably transfers and assigns to [name of assignee] ("Assignee"), located at [address], its successors and assigns, in perpetuity, all right (whether now known or hereinafter invented), title, and interest, throughout the world, including any copyrights and renewals or extensions thereto, in [title and short description of work, including, if available, copyright registration number].

IN WITNESS THEREOF, Assignor has duly executed this Assignment.

[Assignor's name]

By: _____
      [Authorized signature]

Title: _____
      [Assignor's title, e.g., President, Old New Lompoc Co.)

Date: _____

NOTARIZATION [optional]

State of [insert state]

                    SS.:

County of [insert county]

Before me this [date] personally appeared: [name of Assignor], to me known to be the person who is described in and who executed the foregoing Assignment instrument and acknowledged to me that [he/she] executed the same of [his/her] own free will for the purpose therein expressed.

_____
Notary Public

Form I: Permissions Summary Form

Permissions Summary Form Author: _____   Page ___ of ___
Please Type Title: _____   ISBN: _____

Permission Number	Manuscript Page Number	Type of Material Used	SOURCE — Author/Title/Copyright Holder/Copyright Date/Credit Line	Date Requested	Date Granted	Rights Obtained ED	Rights Obtained MKT	Fee	Date Paid	Number of Comp. Copies

Edition Code
This edition only ED
This & future FU
Cloth only CL
Paper only PB
Other* O

Market Code
N. Am. Rights NA
U.S. & Possessions US/P
World Rights (Eng. Lng.) W/E
World Rights (All Lngs.) W
Other* O

*(specify with clear cross-reference to the permission on a separate sheet and attach to form)

Permissions Summary Form: Explanation

Permission number: Number permissions in the order in which the copyrighted items (the first one if a permission covers several) occur in the manuscript or are cited there for later placement.

Manuscript page number: Enter the number of the manuscript page on which the item occurs or is cited for later placement.

Type of material used: Identify the type of material borrowed: text, poetry, table, figure.

Source: Enter the author, publication title, copyright owner, copyright date, and credit data for the borrowed material. Give the credit line that the copyright owner has specified, if any. Include special requirements here.

Date requested: Enter the date on which you requested permission (the date at the top of the Permissions Request form).

Date granted: Enter the date on which permission was granted (the date on which the copyright owner signed the agreement to grant permission).

Rights obtained: Enter the appropriate codes under ED and MKT (the codes are listed at the bottom of the form).

Fee: Enter the fee stipulated by the copyright owner.

Date paid: Date on which the fee was paid. To be entered by the person who pays the fee.

Number of complimentary copies: Enter the number of copies of the published book that the copyright owner has requested.

Form J: Source Notes/Credit Line Form

Page _____ of _____

Author: _____

Title: _____

Permission Number	Manuscript Page Number	Source Notes Author/Title/Copyright Holder/Copyright Date/Credit Line

Instructions: Type double space; triple space between entries.

Note: Credit line entry should follow format specified by copyright holder; if not specified, use standard format.

Form K: Complimentary Copy Form

Page ____ of ____

Author: _____

Title: _____

Per our Permissions agreement, we are contractually obligated to send copies of the above book to the following organizations and/or persons.		Please Type	
Name/Address	# of copies	Name/Address	# of copies

Sample Disclaimers

> **Caution** ⚠ The following is our disclaimer about the use of disclaimers. Disclaimers do not always work. For instance, the fact that an author says that a work is exclusively a work of fiction is not decisive if the reader reasonably believes the work is about a particular living person and it harms that person's reputation.

For Fictional Works

A. This book is a work of fiction. All plots, themes, dates, events, locations, organizations, persons, and characters contained in this material are completely fictional. Any resemblance to any locations, organizations, persons, or characters, real or fictional, living or deceased, is entirely coincidental and unintentional. All characters and character descriptions are products of the author's imagination or are used fictitiously. [Name of publishing company and author] are not responsible for any use of these character names or any resemblance of these character names to actual persons, living or deceased.

B. This book is a work of fiction. Names, characters, places, and incidents either are the product of the author's imagination or are used fictitiously, and any resemblance to actual persons, living or dead, events, or locales is entirely coincidental.

For Partly Fictional Works

A. This book is partly a work of fiction. It is based on a true incident that did occur. However, the names, persons, characters, and dates have been changed and/or fictionalized.

B. This book is a work of fiction, but it was inspired by actual events. All plots, themes, dates, events, locations, organizations, persons, and characters contained in this material are completely fictional. Any resemblance to any locations, organizations, persons, or characters, real or fictional, living or deceased, is entirely coincidental and unintentional.

C. This story is based, in part, on true events, but certain liberties have been taken with names, places, and dates, and the characters have been invented. Therefore, the persons and characters portrayed bear absolutely no resemblance whatever to the persons who were actually involved in the true events described in this story.

For Nonfiction Works

A. This book is intended to provide accurate information with regard to the subject matter covered. However, the author and publisher accept no responsibility for inaccuracies or omissions, and the author and publisher specifically disclaim any liability, loss, or risk, whether personal, financial, or otherwise, that is incurred as a consequence, directly or indirectly, from the use and/or application of any of the contents of this book.

B. This book is intended to provide accurate information. However, in a time of rapid change, it is difficult to ensure that all information provided is entirely accurate and up-to-date. Therefore, the author and the publisher accept no responsibility for any inaccuracies or omissions and specifically disclaim any liability, loss, or risk, personal or otherwise, which is incurred as a consequence, directly or indirectly, of the use and/or application of any of the contents of this book.

C. Readers are strongly cautioned to consult with a physician or other health-care professional before using any information contained in this book. No book can substitute for professional care or advice. Extreme caution is urged when using the information and exercises contained in this book. The author and publisher are not engaging in rendering medical services. If medical problems appear or persist, the reader should consult with a qualified physician or other health-care professional. Accordingly, the author and publisher expressly disclaim any liability, loss, damage, or injury caused by the contents of this book.

Appendix E

Resources

Industry Directories

Advertisers and Advertising Agencies

Standard Directory of Advertisers
Standard Directory of Advertising Agencies
National Register Publishing
P.O. Box 31
New Providence, NJ 07974
800-521-8110 (tel.)

Book Publishing

Literary Market Place (LMP)
International Literary Market Place (ILMP)
Books in Print
International Books in Print
R.R. Bowker
P.O. Box 31
New Providence, NJ 07974
800-521-8110 (tel.)

LMP and its companion volume, ILMP, are annual directories of the book-publishing industry, listing publishing companies, personnel, and services (including picture researchers and permission specialists). *Books in Print* is a master reference to books, authors, and publishers.

Licensing

The Licensing Resource Directory
363 Reef Road
Fairfield, CT 06430
203-256-4700 (tel.)
203-256-4730 (fax)

North American Licensing Industry Buyers Guide
A4 International
41 Madison Avenue
New York, NY 10010

Motion Pictures and Television

Hollywood Creative Directory
3000 West Olympic Boulevard, Suite 2525
Santa Monica, CA 90404-5041
310-315-4816 (tel.)
800-815-0503 (outside CA)

The Hollywood Reporter Blu Book
5055 Wilshire Boulevard, Suite 600
Los Angeles, CA 90036-4396
213-525-2000 (tel.)

NATPE Programmer's Guide
National Association of Television
    Program Executives
10100 Santa Monica Boulevard
Los Angeles, CA 90067
310-453-4440 (tel.)
www.natpe.org

Periodicals

Standard Periodical Directory
Oxbridge Communications, Inc.
105 Fifth Avenue
New York, NY 10011
212-633-2938 (tel.)

Uhlrich's International Periodicals Directory
Working Press of the Nation
R.R. Bowker
P.O. Box 31
New Providence, NJ 07974
800-521-8110 (tel.)

Photography

American Society of Media Photographers
   (ASMP)
Washington Park
14 Washington Road, Suite 502
Princeton Junction, NJ 08550-1033
609-799-8300 (tel.)
www.asmp.org

Picture Agency Council of America
   (PACA)
P.O. Box 308
Northfield, MN 55057-0308
800-457-PACA (7222) (tel.)
www.pacaoffice.org

PACA publishes an annual directory, which cross-references stock photography houses by the types of images they stock.

Visual Arts

AIGA Annual
The American Institute of Graphic Arts
164 Fifth Avenue
New York, NY 10010
212-807-1990 (tel.)
212-807-1799 (fax)

American Showcase
New Media Showcase
915 Broadway, 14th Floor
New York, NY 10010
212-673-6600 (tel.)

Contemporary Artists
Contemporary Designers
St. James Press, a division of
   Gale Research, Inc.
835 Penobscot Bldg.
Detroit, MI 48226-4094
313-961-2242 (tel.)

The Creative Black Book
10 Astor Place, 6th Floor
New York, NY 10003
212-539-9800 (tel.)

The Official Museum Directory
R.R. Bowker
Reed Reference Publishing
P.O. Box 31
New Providence, NJ 07974
800-521-8110 (tel.)

Stock Photo Deskbook
The Photographic Arts Center
163 Amsterdam Avenue
New York, NY 10023
212-838-8640 (tel.)

Trade and Professional Organizations

Advertising Photographers of America
7201 Melrose Avenue
Los Angeles, CA 90046
213-935-2056

American Federation of Musicians
   (AF of M)
1501 Broadway
New York, NY 10036
212-869-1330 (tel.)

American Federation of Television and
    Radio Artists (AFTRA)
6922 Hollywood Boulevard
Hollywood, CA 90028
213-461-8111 (tel.)

American Society of Indexers
P.O. Box 48267
Seattle, WA 98148-0267
206-255-0200 (tel.)

American Society of Journalists and
    Authors (ASJA)
1501 Broadway, Suite 302
New York, NY 10036
212-997-0947 (tel.)
www.asja.org

The American Society of Media
    Photographers, Inc. (ASMP)
Washington Park
14 Washington Road, Suite 502
Princeton Junction, NJ 08550-1033
609-799-8300 (tel.)
www.asmp.org

The American Society of Picture
    Professionals (ASPP)
2025 Pennsylvania Avenue NW, #226
Washington, DC 20006
202-955-5578 (tel.)
www.S2f.com/stockphoto

Art Information Center (AIC)
55 Mercer Street
New York, NY 10003
212-966-3443 (tel.)

Association of American Publishers (AAP)
1718 Connecticut Avenue, NW
Washington, DC 20009
202-232-3335 (tel.)
www.publishers.org

The Authors Guild
330 West 42nd Street, 29th Floor
New York, NY 10036
212-563-5904 (tel.)

The Directors Guild of America (DGA)
7920 Sunset Boulevard
Los Angeles, CA 90046
310-289-2000 (tel.)

The Dramatists Guild
234 West 44th Street, 11th Floor
New York, NY 10036
212-398-9366 (tel.)

Editorial Freelancers Association (EFA)
71 West 23rd Street, Suite 1504
New York, NY 10010
212-929-5400 (tel.)

Graphic Artists Guild (GAG)
90 John Street
New York, NY 10038-3202
212-791-0330 (tel.)
www.gag.org

Licensing Industry Merchandisers'
    Association (LIMA)
350 Fifth Avenue, Suite 2309
New York, NY 10118-6293
212-244-1944 (tel.)

Motion Picture Screen Cartoonists Union
    (MPSC)
4729 Lankershim Boulevard
North Hollywood, CA 91602-1864
818-766-7151 (tel.)

National Cartoonists Society (NCS)
10 Columbus Circle, #1620
New York, NY 10019
212-627-1550

National Writers Union (NWU)
113 University Place
New York, NY 10003
212-254-0279 (tel.)
www.nwu.org/nwu

PEN American Center
568 Broadway
New York, NY 10012-3225
212-334-1660 (tel.)

Picture Agency Council of America
(PACA)
P.O. Box 308
Northfield, MN 55057-0308
800-457-PACA (7222) (tel.)

Publishers Marketing Association (PMA)
627 Aviation Way
Manhattan Beach, CA 90266
310-372-2732 (tel.)
www.pma-online.org

Screen Actors Guild (SAG)
5757 Wilshire Boulevard
Los Angeles, CA 90036-3600
213-954-1600 (tel.)

Society of Children's Book Writers &
Illustrators (SCBWI)
22736 Vanowen Street, Suite 106
West Hills, CA 91307
818-888-8760 (tel.)
www.scbwi.org

Software Publishers Association (SPA)
1730 M Street NW, Suite 700
Washington, DC 20036-4510
202-452-1600 (tel.)
www.spa.org

Text and Academic Authors Association,
Inc. (TAA)
Koquina Hall, #234
140 Seventh Avenue South
University of South Florida–St. Petersberg
St. Petersberg, FL 33701
813-553-1195 (tel.)

Toy Manufacturers of America
200 Fifth Avenue, Suite 740
New York, NY 10010
212-675-1141 (tel.)

Writers Guild of America, East, Inc.
(WGA, East)
555 West 57th Street
New York, NY 10019
212-767-7800 (tel.)

Writers Guild of America, West, Inc.
(WGA, West)
7000 West Third Street
Los Angeles, CA 90048
310-550-1000 (tel.)
www.wga.org

Copyright Licensing Organizations

Authors

The Authors Registry
330 West 42nd Street
New York, NY 10036
212-563-6920 (tel.)
registry@interport.com (E-mail)
www.webcom.com/registry

Copyright Clearance Center (CCC)
222 Rosewood Drive
Danvers, MA 01923
508-750-8400 (tel.)
508-750-4744 (fax)
www.copyright.com

The CCC is a photocopying clearinghouse
that collects license fees for photocopying of
books, journals, newsletters, newspapers, and
scientific monographs.

Publication Rights Clearinghouse (PRC)
National Writers Union (NWU)/West
Coast Office
337 17th Street, Suite 101
Oakland, CA 94612
510-839-0110 (tel.)

The Publication Rights Clearinghouse (PRC)
is the National Writers Union's (NWU)
online royalty collection agency for freelance
writers. The NWU and the UnCover Company, an NWU licensee, maintain an online,
transaction-based article-delivery system,
which clears copyrights and collects royalties
for fax-delivery orders.

Photographers

Media Photographers' Copyright Agency
   (MP©A)
Washington Park
14 Washington Road, Suite 502
Princeton Junction, NJ 08550-1033
609-799-8300 (tel.)

MP©A acts as a licensing agent for photographers and provides digital delivery of stock images. The agency also acts as a referral agency for nonparticipating ASMP members and their representatives.

Songwriters

ASCAP: Los Angeles
7920 Sunset Boulevard
Los Angeles, CA 90046
213-883-1000 (tel.)

ASCAP: New York
One Lincoln Plaza
New York, NY 10023
212-595-3050 (tel.)
www.ascap.com

BMI: Los Angeles
8730 Sunset Boulevard
Los Angeles, CA 90069
310-659-9109 (tel.)

BMI: New York
320 West 57th Street
New York, NY 10019
212-586-2000 (tel.)
www.bmi.com

Society of European Stage Actors and
   Composers (SESAC)
421 West 54th Street
New York, NY 10019
212-586-3450 (tel.)

The ASCAP and BMI song-title databases allow researchers to search by song, title, songwriter, or publisher for information on songs and songwriters registered with these performing-rights societies. If you don't know which society a writer belongs to, look at the liner notes that accompanied the CD or cassette. If a songwriter isn't registered with ASCAP, there's an excellent chance he or she is affiliated with BMI. If all else fails, contact SESAC.

Harry Fox Agency, Inc.
and
National Music Publishers' Assoc., Inc.
711 Third Avenue
New York, NY 10017
212-370-5330 (tel.)

Visual Artists

Artists Rights Society (ARS)
65 Bleeker Street
New York, NY 10012
212-420-9160 (tel.)

Visual Artists and Galleries Association
   (VAGA)
521 Fifth Avenue, Suite 800
New York, NY 10017
212-808-0616 (tel.)

ARS and VAGA are artists' rights organizations that license reproduction rights to users of visual art on behalf of their members. ARS represents the estates of many of the artists active in France in this century, including Kandinsky, Braque, Chagall, and Miró. VAGA represents thousands of artists worldwide, from struggling artists to well-known names such as Robert Motherwell and Larry Rivers.

Voluntary Legal Assistance

Volunteer Lawyers for the Arts
1 East 53rd Street, 6th Floor
New York, NY 10022
212-319-2787 (tel.)

Copyright and Trademark Search Firms

Government Liaison Services, Inc.
3030 Claredon Boulevard, Suite 209
Arlington, VA 22201
800-642-6564 (tel.)

NatPatco, Ltd.
P.O. Box 1631
Morristown, NJ 07960
800-221-6275 (tel.)

Thomson & Thomson
1750 K Street NW, Suite 200
Washington, DC 20006-2305
800-356-8630 (tel.)
www.thomson-thomson.com

XL Corporate Services
62 White Street
New York, NY 10013
800-221-2972 (tel.)

Miscellaneous

*The Mini-Encyclopedia of Public Domain
    Songs*
BZ/Rights & Permissions, Inc.
125 West 72nd Street
New York, NY 10023
212-580-0615 (tel.)

The Public Domain Report Monthly
P.O. Box 3102
Margate, NJ 08402
800-827-9401 (tel.)

About the Authors

Lloyd J. Jassin specializes in copyright, trademark, publishing, television, and multimedia law. He has written extensively on negotiating contracts in the publishing and entertainment industries, and lectures frequently around the country on entertainment and media law topics. Mr. Jassin is a member of the Board of Directors of the Small Press Center. He was formerly associated with Viacom Enterprises, where he was involved in television production, distribution, and celebrity licensing. Before becoming an attorney, he was Director of Publicity for the Simon & Schuster Reference Group. He practices law in New York City and is a member of the New York and New Jersey bars.

Steven C. Schechter practices law in Fair Lawn, New Jersey, and in New York City. Mr. Schechter's practice includes the areas of motion picture, television, and publishing law, and he also handles libel and first amendment litigation. He is admitted to practice law in New York, New Jersey, and the District of Columbia, and he serves as a Commissioner on the New Jersey Motion Picture and Television Development Commission. Mr. Schechter has taught courses on entertainment and publishing law at Rutgers University and at Seton Hall University School of Law and lectures throughout the country on media law topics.